COMMON
DENOMINATORS TO SUCCESS

COMMON DENOMINATORS TO SUCCESS

Humphrey Mutiti

CM PUBLISHERS (CANADA)

TORONTO, CANADA – 2016

Common Denominators to Success

Copyright © 2016 by Humphrey Mutiti. All rights reserved.

No part of this book may be reproduced, stored in a retrieval system of transmitted, in any form or by any means, electronic, mechanical, photocopying or otherwise, without the prior written permission of the publisher.

All scripture quotations are from the Holy Bible, King James Version, or otherwise indicated; used by permission.

PUBLISHED BY:

CM PUBLISHERS (CANADA)
6 Milvan Drive, Suite 303/305 | Toronto, Ontario M9L 1Z2
CANADA

CM PUBLISHERS (CANADA)publishes works of less known talented authors worldwide in order to make them known.

Book design copyright © 2016 by CM PUBLISHERS (Canada). All rights reserved.

Cover Design: PowerBrain Studio (Republic of South Africa)
Interior Design: CM Publishers (Canada)

PUBLISHED IN CANADA;

ISBN-13: 978-1-988251-03-5; ISBN-10: 1988251036

Spiritual,
Success & Failure
16.04.30

Dedication

To my lovely wife, Felicite.

Thank you. Without your support and patience, I would have never achieved my dream.

Contents

Acknowledgements viii
Foreword ix
Introduction 1
Chapter 1: Power of a Vision 3
Chapter 2: Mystery of Failure 19
Chapter 3: Power of Focus 29
Chapter 4: Power of Passion 41
Chapter 5: Power of Discipline 49
Chapter 6: Associations 55
Chapter 7: Hard Work 63
Chapter 8: Price of Criticism 71
Chapter 9: Test of Submission 79
Chapter 10: Getting Out of Debt 99
Chapter 11: God Factor 115
Index 123
Notes 128

Acknowledgements

I would like to thank the congregation at Covenant Church International (CCI), South Africa, and my family, without whose help this book would never have been completed.

I am deeply indebted to Professor Charles Mwewa, and who is also my spiritual father. He took me in when no-one knew who and what I was and his encouragement and commitment to me and my vision across the years have not diminished.

Thank you, Brother John Ebo Opare from CCI, for helping with the cover design and impressions.

Thank you, Mr. Serge Adande, for your parental care, advice and every support you have always given to me in every way.

Many thanks to Mr. Sumani Enerst and Mr. Alex Samulatunga, your support and care enabled me to bless many.

Last, but not least, I extend my heartfelt gratitude to the following: Rev. Larry Odonkor; Bishop John Mnvik; Pastor Isaac Machisa; Pastor Fredrick Nkansah; and Mum Emily, for being tremendous blessings in my life.

Foreword

I am deeply honoured to pen a foreword to this illustrious book by Pastor Humphrey Mutiti. The challenge that all will encounter, perhaps, is the one to do with failure. And it is no wonder the author immediately takes us to Chapter 2 after discussing Vision in Chapter 1. We are prepared to succeed. We are told just when we reach the age of reason that success is good. We also observe what *successful* people do and what they have. We develop a knack for success, and will do all and everything to "succeed."

However, do we even know what success is? This book tells us what true success is. The author draws from his own life experiences and the wisdom he has garnered from God and the Word to solicitously advocate for thorough understanding in regards to the nature of success.

In mathematics a common denominator essentially absorbs all the enumerable components. It is common to all even if respective numbers may differ in value or quantity. Differ they may, but they will be united in the fact that one thing connects them all. This is, then referred to as a common denominator. Success is the same. All those who have succeeded had one or an aggregate of the factors discussed in this book. This is one of the reasons why this book is unique. The author invites us to go no further – to stay close to the author's generosity offered through the pages of this book. I have gone through every chapter, paragraph by paragraph and I have grown. You are guaranteed to grow after reading this book.

I have known the author practically all his life. He did not acquire this glorious mentality from reading other people's treatise or sampling through professionally crafted literature available in the marketplace. He acquired these principles from a very hard and tough journey towards the top. The author has personally suffered loss, defeat and rejection and has emerged from them even stronger. This author chose to believe in the God of miracles and of second chances. Today, he stands as a testimony of God's wisdom, faithfulness and patience. Because he has been there, and he overcame and continued to fight and conquer, of course, with the help of God, what he writes in this book is practical and authentic.

I strongly recommend this book to everyone; especially to those who believe that God has called them to something greater than themselves!

> Charles Mwewa,
> *Author, legal professor, leader, intercessor*
> Canada
> April 2016

Introduction

There is nothing in life that is more widely admired than success. Success is intentional. No one succeeds by chance. Success does not just happen. In real life, success comes after hard work and discipline; it proceeds from a vision. It entails sacrifice, and it is failure's brainchild. Success does not happen instantaneously. It must be initiated. It must be worked for. Sometimes one will need to sweat for it or pay for it. Anyone who has succeeded in life, had to pay for it in some way. In this book, I will share some of the common denominators that you will find at least in almost everyone who has made it in the sphere of business, ministry, academics and any area of their lives. Yet, this author insists that true success has to involve God.

It is said that success is doing well in life. I want to add that success is doing well in any field of your life, in gift or in career. Success is making it. It is progressing. It is achieving your dream. Success is not only monetary but it includes many areas of life. One can be successful health-wise or financially. One can also be successful in business, in ministry, in talent, in politics or in building oneself.

In 1 Corinthians 9:24-27, we read: "Know ye not that they which run in a race run all, but one recieveth the prize? So run, that ye may obtain. And every man that striveth for the mastery is temperate in all things. Now they do it to obtain a corruptible crown; but we an incorruptible. I therefore so run, not as un-certainly; so fight I, not as one that beateth the air: But I keep under my body, and bring it into subjection: least that by any means, when I have preached to others, I myself should be castaway," (Holy Bible, King James Version).

In reference to the above passage of Scripture, I reiterate the Apostle Paul's words, "In a race all the runners run, but only one gets a prize." In this life we are all in a race in whatever sphere we are operating. Life is a race. This is why in the same life others are making it, and others are not. Same business, others are making it and others are not. Same environment, others are failing and others are succeeding. Same ministry, others are making it and others are failing. It is this secret which makes others to shine and the journey it has taken me to become what I have become, which partly compelled me to write this book.

As you follow me through this book, you will discover the secrets why a few people thrive in various aspects of their endeavours whiles the majority does not.

Chapter 1: Power of a Vision

"Where there is no vision, people cast off restraint; but he that keepeth the law, happy is he," (Proverbs 29:18).

A study of successful people will reveal that they all had a personal vision. They all had what they wanted to achieve. They were not doing everything but they were doing something. They all had something they wanted to achieve. It's impossible to succeed in life without a vision.

A vision is neither a dream that one has at night nor a trance. A vision is a master-plan of your life. It is a blue-print of your life. It is a sense of sight. It is a purpose of your life. A vision is seeing what God has in mind for you. A vision is God's personal instruction to you. A vision is the unfolding of divine plan and purpose for your life. A vision is a portrait of your future. A vision is what God wants you to be. A vision is a discovery for which you are created for. It is the reason you are living. The idea of a vision is reinforced in the following verses of Scriptures:

"And the Lord answered me, and said, write the vision, and make it plain upon tablets, that he may run that readeth it. For the vision is yet for an appointed time, but at the end it shall speak and not lie: though it tarry, wait for it; because it will surely come, it will not tarry," (Habakkuk 2:2-3).

"Before I formed thee in the belly I knew thee; and before thou comest forth out of the womb I sanctified thee, and I ordained thee a prophet unto the nations," (Jeremiah 1:5).

God revealed His purpose for creating Prophet Jeremiah. Thus, a vision is what God had ordained you to be unto the nations. In this life, some are ordained to be pastors, business men and women, medical doctors, entrepreneurs, footballers, singers, teachers, mentors, instructors and the list is endless. I want you to know that you cannot amount to anything without knowing who you are. You cannot amount to anything without knowing what God has ordained you to be unto the nations. You need to know your identity. You need to know who you are. You need to know what God has wired you for. You need to know why God made you – "But when it pleased God, who separated me from my mother's womb, and called me by His grace, to reveal his Son in me, that I might preach Him among the heathen…" (Galatians 1:15-16).

Jeremiah's purpose was to be a prophet and Paul's was to preach to the heathen. You also have a purpose for being here on earth. That purpose for your being here on earth is what is called a vision. A vision may be, therefore, defined as knowing what you are here on earth for.

It is very important that you discover what your vision is, because this may put an end to a life of struggles. This may stop you from being a stranger to yourself. You may keep struggling when God's plan for your life is unknown, because you are designed to perform best at the assignment you are created to perform, just as any product only functions optimally when used for the purpose that it was specifically designed for. A man without a vision may be a frustrated in life.

A vision is God's master-plan of your life; ambition is man-made

A vision is God-given, whereas ambition is man-made. Vision is from above, while ambition has its origin here on earth. Ambition is born out of earthly drive to do it better than others. It springs mostly out of envy and a desire for power and self-recognition. These desires may run so deeply that men fix their eyes on their target and go all out to achieve it, using all means, including all manner of evil conspiracies. Men obsessed by their ambition can kill, destroy nations and cities and pull others down, just to achieve their goal. Somebody once said, "Men with ambition have PHDs – or 'Pull Him Down' mentality."

Look at Hitler who was a man of ambition. He wanted to rule the world. He wanted the

Germany nation to bear rule over the whole world and felt that the Jews were in the way of his actualizing this, so he decided to exterminate them. Hitler had an ambition and nothing was too evil for him to do to achieve it.

But the great man of faith, George Muller, had a vision, a heavenly dream. He wanted to put a smile on the faces of all the orphans left by the war. He gave up everything he had to start an orphanage, looking unto God alone for help. He did not have to steal, kill or beg people for sustenance. It is a vision that separates men from boys – "For as the heavens are higher than the earth, so are my ways higher than your ways, and my thoughts than your thoughts," (Isaiah 55:9).

When you walk by the high ways of God, you become a high flyer in life – "And it shall come to pass and, if thou shalt hearken diligently unto the voice of the Lord thy God, to observe and to do all His commandments which I command thee this day, that the Lord thy God *will set thee on high above all nations on earth*," (Deuteronomy 28:1, emphasis added).

When you pursue the mind of God concerning your life, He makes you to be a high flyer. God sets you on high above all the nations.

There are few points I want to share with you about the vision. It is these points that will help you to know if what you have is either a vision or an ambition. I see God helping you discover your vision! I see you running with your vision and fulfilling it!

(a) *A vision originates from God*

"Before I formed thee in the belly I knew thee; and before thou camest forth out of the womb I sanctified thee, and I ordained thee a prophet unto the nations," (Jeremiah 1:5).

God is your manufacturer and you are His product. He is the only one who knows who you are. He is the one who knows your use. This is why everyone who has succeeded in life will tell you they discovered who they were and pursued their vision. Your pastor does not know who you are. Your parents do not know who you are, either. Your boss at work does not know who you either. Only God knows who you are. He is the only one who knows your purpose. If you are to succeed in life, you will need to discover who you are and what you can do best. Sometimes, God may reveal your vision through a prophecy, a dream like He did to Joseph, through circumstances of life or through His Word.

(b) *A vision from God is always new*

"For in Christ Jesus neither circumcision availeth anything, nor uncircumcision but a new creature," (Galatians 6:15).

Whenever God starts something, it is always new and of its kind. It is not second-hand or a photocopy. Every man who has succeeded in life had to start a new thing. He had to start from the base. Very few people, if any, who inherited something, have succeeded. I have seen businesses fall apart when the one who started them dies. I have seen churches fall apart when the visionary dies. And I have also seen political parties crumble down when its founder dies.

Consider the following Scriptures:

"Behold, I will do a new thing; now it shall spring forth..." (Isaiah 43:19).

"But as it is written, eye has not seen, nor ear heard, neither have it entered into the heart of man, the things which God hath prepared for them that love Him," (1 Corinthians 2:9).

God is your manufacturer and you are His product. Usually, when you ask God for your vision, He may tell you to start from the scratch. I believe God does this to make us grow with our vision. In this way, we can grow with the vision. He would want you to grow with your church. He would want you to grow with your company. He would want you to grow with your political party or your gift. Of course, there will be challenges here and there, but you will need to be faithful in the little, and the Lord will entrust you with much. Manage the little you have, and the Lord will give you the increase.

Consider:

"Though thy beginnings were small, yet thy latter end should greatly increase," (Job 8:7), and

"For who hath despised the day of small things?" (Zechariah 4:10)!

In my ministry and life, I have met many people who want to be great and yet they are not taking care of the little they have. Even in the business world, you will notice that you are only promoted when you prove to be more productive at the small present-day position. Do you want to pastor a big church? Do you want to have a big business? Do you want to achieve much in life? The answer is in taking care of the little you have and you will soon climb the ladder of success.

(c) *A vision will set out a goal to achieve*

"Where there is no vision, the people perish: but he that keepeth the law, happy is he," (Proverbs 29:18).

A vision will condition you. It will determine your behaviour. It will also determine how you spend your money and the type of friends you will choose. A vision will compel you to make a budget when you are paid. Somebody once said, "Show me your friends and I will tell you your future."

A vision will dictate your life. You do not need a pastor to tell you what you are doing is wrong, all you need is a vision and it will put your life in line. You do not need the police to tell you that what you are doing is against the laws of the land, the vision will tell you. A vision is like a thermometer that will let you know when your temperature is high. A vision is like the road signs on your way to success. A vision will keep your head high.

(d) *A vision will keep you alive*

"And there came thither certain Jews from Antioch and Iconium, who persuaded the people, and, having stoned Paul, drew him out of the city, supposing he had been dead. Howbeit, as the disciples stood round about him, he rose up, and came into the city: and the next day he departed with Barnabas to Derbe," (Acts 14:19-20).

God made sure he preserved Paul's life so that he could accomplish his dream. The Apostle Paul faced death daily but he never died until he accomplished his vision. Even when many times he was beaten and left to die, he did not die because he had not fulfilled his vision yet. May God preserve your life until you fulfil your dream, in the name of Jesus!

Moses could not die until he accomplished his vision. Elijah never died until he accomplished his vision. Jesus never died until he accomplished his vision. David never died until he accomplished his vision. Noah did not die until he accomplished his vision. May this be your story as well! I say you will not die before your dream is fulfilled! No sickness, accident or *sangoma* (witchdoctor) will take your life until you fulfil your destiny in the name of Jesus!

Lastly, allow me to end this chapter by showing you how you can fulfil your vision. Because if you do not know how to run with your vision, you may not see it coming to pass:

COMMON DENOMINATORS TO SUCCESS

(i) *Divine guidance*

One of the greatest tragedies of life is to lack the knowledge of where you are going as well as not knowing how to get there. Since God created you to perform a specific task, then He should be allowed to show you how it should be done. A manufacturer is the one who knows best what he designed a product to perform, and that's why every product comes with a manufacturer's manual which tells you how to use it. God is the only one who can tell you what your use in this life is.

While vision shows you the Promised Land, God's guidance is what enables you to arrive there. God's guidance gives you the means to get there: "And it came to pass, when Pharaoh had let people go, that God led them through the way of the land of the Philistines, although that was near; for God said, Let peradventure the people repent when they see war, and they return to Egypt: But God led the people about, through the way of the wilderness of the Red Sea: and the children of Israel went up harnessed out of the land of Egypt," (Exodus 13:17-18).

Since it was God who made us and not us ourselves, it is essential that we look up to Him to show us the way to fulfil our vision – "There is a way which seemeth right unto man, but the end thereof are the ways of death," (Proverbs 14:12).

It is God's leading that makes the journey of life great. The Bible commands that we walk not by sight, but by faith (2 Corinthians 5:7). Following divine guidance is a supernatural distinguish-distinguishing mark of every follower: "Follow me, and I will make you…" (Matthew 4:19). This means that your making is in *the* following. God is saying, "Allow me to lead you, and I will make you what I have created you to be." When you are following His plan, you commit His integrity to backing you up, because, "Faithful is He that calleth you, who also will do it," (1 Thess. 5:24).

Following God's guidance leads to true prosperity: "And he shall be like a tree planted by the river of water, that bringeth forth his fruits in his season, his leaf also shall not wither; *and whatever he doeth shall prosper*," (Psalm 1:3, emphasis added). The greatest leader that ever walked the face of the earth, Jesus Christ the Son of God, said, "I can of my own self do nothing: as I hear, I judge; and my judgement is just," (John 5:30).

God guided Moses: "And the Lord went before them by day in a pillar of cloud, to lead them the way; and by night in a pillar of fire, to give them light; to go by the day and night. He took away not the pillar of the cloud by day, not the pillar of fire by night, from before the people," (Exodus 13:21-22). The Israelites journeyed for forty years through the wilderness by divine signal. They only moved by divine signals, is there any wonder then that they arrived at the Promised Land or that there was not one feeble person among them in forty years of travelling through rough terrain? (Numbers 9:15-23)

God is committed in guiding us if only we are committed to following Him. He will not force us to follow Him:

> And it came to pass, that, as they went in the way, a certain man said unto Him, Lord, I will follow thee withersoever thou goest. And Jesus said unto him, Foxes have holes, and birds of the air have nests; but the Son of man hath not where to lay his head. And he said unto another, Follow me. But he said, Lord, suffer me first to go and bury my father. Jesus said unto him, let the dead bury their dead: but go thou and preach the Kingdom of God. And another also said, Lord, I will follow thee; but let me first go bid them farewell, which are at home at my house. And Jesus said unto him, No man, having put his hand to the plough, and looking back, is fit for the kingdom of God (Luke 9:57-62).

Following God's guidance is a choice: "Remember the former things of old; for I am God, and there is none else: I am God, and there is none like me, declaring the end from the beginning and from ancient times the things that are not yet done, saying, My counsel shall stand, and I will do all my pleasure," (Isaiah 46:9-10).

(ii) *Correct timing*

"To everything there is a season, and a time to every purpose under the heaven," (Ecclesiastes 3:1).

If you are to fulfil your vision, you will need to move at the appointed time into every phase of your vision. Timing is very important in life. When you get to the airport late, you will miss your flight. You will be at the right airport, but because your timing is wrong, you will miss your flight. Many people are doing the right things at the wrong times or doing the wrong things at the right place. This leads to disaster and frustration in life. Follow the time for your dream because every vision is for an appointed time. There is always a set time to step out in fulfilling a vision. When you step out at the right time to fulfil your vision God makes all things beautiful: "He has made everything beautiful in his time," (Ecclesiastes 3:11).

Whatever God has shown you to do has also a time He wants you do it. Every vision has its time to be fulfilled. Do not be comfortable overstaying where you are: "Arise ye, and depart; for this is not your rest: because it is polluted, it shall destroy you, even with a sore destruction," (Micah 2:10). Also, "The Lord our God spoke unto us in Horeb, saying, Ye have dwelt long enough in this mountain; Turn you, and take your journey...." (Deuteronomy 1:6-7), and "Ye have compassed this mountain long enough: turn you northward..." (Deuteronomy 2:3).

Every vision has its time to be fulfilled. We need to be sensitive to divine plan and programme, so we can keep pace with God. That way we will not overstay in a phase and stand the risk of losing our place. Our path in life is ordained to shine brighter and brighter, "But the path of the just is as the shining light, that shineth more and more unto the perfect day," (Proverbs 4:18). That means that we are expected to move from phase to phase in our journey in life.

(iii) *Security of destiny*

For forty years that the children travelled through the wilderness, none among them was feeble, and their legs were not swollen. This was because they were constantly moving with the cloud, which was their covering during the day and pillar of fire in the night. As a result, no killer beast could dare come near them. Not one person was feeble among them, because the cloud of the glory guided and covered them. The cloud moved from day to day. Every time the cloud moved, the people moved, and whenever it stopped, they stopped.

Where you are now is not your end. God said, "You will still bring fourth fruit even in old age," (Psalm 92:14). This means that God is not done with you until you draw your last breath.

Chapter 2: Mystery of Failure

“For a just man falleth seven times, and riseth up again: but the wicked shall fall into mischief," (Proverbs 24:16).

A journey to success will take you through many routes, which sometimes may be through failure. Somebody once noted, "You can't travel a road to success without a puncture or two."

People who have succeeded in life had failures at one time. This is why success is built from the ashes of failure. If you are to succeed in this life you will need to know how to handle failure. Because it is not the failing that matters, but what you do when you fail. What matters is what happens after the fall. It is said that, "Failure is not in the failing but in the staying down." Failure is not a person but an event. I have always told our church that when you fail it means you are only knocked down and not out of the ring. Thus, you are not out of the ring. You can bounce back with a difference if you decide to.
Failure is normal and I believe you need it in life. Many of the success stories have been born from the ashes of failure. Failure is a back door to success.

COMMON DENOMINATORS TO SUCCESS

The great leaders we have today mastered how to handle failure. Many times failure brings pain, sorrow and a sense of despair. It may even lead to being a laughing stock of the people. And this makes failure such a terrible experience in a person's life. Failure may also bring with it loss of privileges and respect in society because only those who succeed are applauded, esteemed, flattered and admired. Failure may be a dishonourable experience.

Let us look at a man who failed countless times and yet still made it to the top. This man knew how to handle failure squarely. We are told he essentially became one of the best presidents of the United States of America. I believe his became one of the best presidencies because he failed several times in life so he had so much experience and knowledge to avoid further failure.

Abraham Lincoln:

In 1831 – He lost his job
1832 – He was defeated in the run for Illinois State Legislature
1833 – He failed in business
1834 – Elected into Illinois State Legislature (Success)
1835 – Sweetheart died.
1836 – Had nervous breakdown.

1838 – Defeated in the run for Illinois House Speaker.
1843 – Defeated in the run for nomination for U.S. Congress.
1846 – Elected to Congress (Success).
1848 – Lost re – nomination.
1849 – Rejected for land officer position.
1854 – Defeated in the run for U.S. Senate.
1856 – Defeated in the run for nomination for Vice-president.
1858 – Again defeated in the run for U.S. Senate.
1860 – Elected president (Success).

He started striving for success when he was twenty two years and only made it when he was fifty one years. The man had many set-backs but he kept his faith and dream until he made it to the White House.

Paul Galvin, at the age of thirty-three had failed twice in business. With his last $750, he bought back the battery eliminator portion of it. That part became Motorola. Upon his retirement in the 1960's, he said, "Do not fear mistakes. You will know failure. Continue to reach out."

I want to believe that a life spent making mistakes is more useful than a life spent doing nothing.

Failure is a situation, never a person.

Many times people will fail for no fault of their own. They fail because of circumstances beyond their control. Some people are themselves to blame for their failure, because they lack discipline, understanding of times and sometimes they do not want to learn. They are too stubborn to be taught. Other times people also fail because they are so puffed up that they do not want to ask. They have pride that only lifts them to bring them down.

You need to understand that failure will come on your way to success whether you like it or not. My spiritual father Professor Charles Mwewa once said, "So the question should not be, 'Will I one day fail?' Instead it should be 'What will I do when I one day fail?'"

Do not be cheated that you will not fail or make mistakes in life. Ask the people who have succeeded in life, they will tell you that they failed many times. It is only that we met them after they had succeeded. We only met them after they had known their spouse. Always remember that before they knew each other at one time, it was Jim and Jack.

My personal philosophy in life is that only those who have failed many times are the people who have much to offer in life. They are the ones who become the best teachers. A man who has never failed somewhere, that man cannot begreat.

One of my sons in the Lord one time asked me whether I have had failures in life and ministry. I told him I have had many failures and failure has taught me a lot of things in life. Failure is the best teacher.

For you to know how to handle and turn failure into success, you must first know how to handle it. You need to know that:

1. Failure is common to all of us

"For a just man falleth seven times, and riseth up again…" (Proverbs 24:16).

Many people give up when they fail because they personalise it and feel so ashamed to raise up and try again. Never forget that you are not the first one to fail. Never also forget that there is someone somewhere who is making it in the same area of life you have failed. Thus, stop having pity for yourself and rise up.

2. Failure is not a respecter of persons

Failure has no size. I have seen the old and young fail. I have seen Whites as well as Blacks fail. I have seen the great and small fail. I have seen the mighty and the weak fail. I have seen the rich and the poor fail. There is no exception to failure. This is why you need to know how to handle failure because it will definitely come one day. You need to know that everyone has potential to fail.

Thomas Edison, the man who invented the light bulb was asked by a reporter how many times he failed before he finally succeeded in making a bulb, we are told he answered (rephrased), "I never failed but I only learnt the ways in which it did not work."

Failure is not final. Keep trying child of God. Keep trying my sister. Keep trying my brother. Keep going. All the padlocks you see have their own keys. If the key you have is not opening the door, try using other keys and the door will eventually open. You say, "I wish you knew how many times I have failed in my relationship. I wish you knew how many times I have failed in my business." I wish you can see God's grace available for you to make you succeed in life. This time around you will not fail! This time it will work out in the name of Jesus! This time around your business will thrive, in the name of Jesus!

3. Failure is part of the learning curve

You cannot climb a ladder of success without encountering failure in one way or another. Failure is a subject in the school of success. It is a topic in the school of success. It is a subject that all of us should take. Great men have learnt how to handle failure. They have learnt how to take failure as a lesson in life. Use failure to learn what to avoid next time in order to succeed. When you make mistakes, just learn from them. Mistakes are often the best teachers.

4. **Failure helps you to improve**

Sometimes failure will help you to improve. It will help you to change. It will help you to check your life. It will help you to take stock of your life. It will help you evaluate your life and see where you need to make adjustments. Failure will give you time to think, rest and even come up with good plans to prevail. It will sometimes make you wise. Show me a man who has failed before and I will show you a successful man.

5. **Failure may make you depend on God**

Failure sometimes will cause you to depend on God's grace. I have noticed that when you fail, it forces you to humble yourself and depend on God. This is why it is so impossible for a man who has had many failures in life when he succeeds to have pride or take the glory in his success. Failure will compel you to realise that it is God who deserves to be praised in your business, ministry, marriage and life.

6. Failure brings compassion

Failure will force you feel sorry for others and do something to comfort them. It will make you have love and mercy for others. You will not rejoice in the failure of others. You will not celebrate in their failure but you will always find a way of becoming their strength. You will always try to be a pillar of strength from where they can lean – "Wherefore let him that thinketh he standeth take heed lest he fall," (1 Corinthians 10:12). Failure may be delay, but not defeat. It is a temporary detour, and not a dead end street.

7. Failure is written in pencil, not in ink

Failure is not perpetual. Failing is not a problem but it is failing to get up that is a problem. I do not know who is reading this book, but whoever you are, this is your message. God shall restore you and make you a success. It is not over yet until God says so. You are not a loser until you win. I see you making it from this day on wards. Where others failed, you will succeed.

8. Failure will keep you humble

Sometimes God may allow us to fail in order to humble us. Have you ever seen a man who has just failed in life or an exam? Many times they become humble. They are ready to listen. They are ready to be corrected.

A journey to success will take you through many routes, which sometimes may be through failure. Success is built from the ashes of failure. It is not the failing that matters, but what you do when you fail. What matters is what happens after the fall. Failure is not in the failing but in the staying down. Failure is normal and I believe you need it in life. Many of the success stories have been born from the ashes of failure. Failure is a back door to success. The great leaders we have today have mastered how to handle failure.

Chapter 3: Power of Focus

"Brethren, I count not myself to have apprehended: but this one thing I do, forgetting those things which are behind, and reaching forth unto those things which are before. I press toward the mark for the prize of high calling of God in Christ Jesus," (Philippians 3:13-14).

Brother Paul tells us that the secret in his success has been forgetting the past and pressing on towards his vision. Similarly, you cannot make it in life without vision. And an important aspect of vision you will need is focus. You will need focus in ministry. You will need focus to succeed in your marriage, business and whatever you are doing in life. There is power in focus. Many people in ministry have the anointing but they have no focus. Many people can thrive in business but they lack focus. Many people can do well in politics but they lack focus; they are busy jumping from one political party to another. Many people can go very far in life but they lack focus.

Focus is the ability to direct attention at something. It is an aptitude to direct one's efforts on one thing. It is a capability to concentrate on one thing and stay committed to it. To have focus is to have a single commitment. Focus is the target you want to reach in your life.

Every stage of human development requires focus. An athlete, a student, a man or woman in love, a pastor, a politician, a political party to win and form a government will need focus. It is focus that will differentiate between success and failure, between progress and stagnation, between victory and defeat. Focus is what will propel you forwards and motivate you to fulfil your destiny. It is focus that will catapult you to your destiny.

Many people have gifts that can make them cause waves on earth but because they lack focus, they have made no impact and no one knows about them. They cannot stay at one job, they are always changing companies. They are always changing businesses and changing careers. They are always changing goal posts. If you are to succeed in this life, you will need to be focused. You will need to be committed to your vision. Do not allow people or things in this life to distract you from your purpose.

The following three factors will be required in order to remain focused.

1. The Devil

"And conspired all of them together to come and to fight against Jerusalem, and to hinder it," (Nehemiah 4:8).

What Sanballat did was to try to cause a detour to Nehemiah and the Israelites. Sanballat wanted the Israelites to stop building the walls of Jerusalem; he wanted them to waste time fighting him. But Nehemiah knew exactly what he wanted and refused to be distracted: "And it came to pass, when our enemies heard that it was known unto us, and God had brought their counsel to nought, that we returned all of us to the wall, everyone unto his work," (Nehemiah 4:15).

It is not every event in life that you can go to. Some of the events are Sanballats that the devil brings to detour you from your purpose in life. A pastor cannot allow the enemy to detour him on a Saturday by going partying till 9p.m instead of seeking God's face to prepare himself for Sunday. The devil is the principal of distraction. If the devil cannot get you to sin, he will distract you. The devil can create a detour and take you off the main road as it is commonly done in road construction. Now you need to understand the characteristics of a detour. It is a road you can travel on but it is not good because:

(a) *It is mostly a temporary road*

It is not permanent. You may not find it tomorrow. You may be on a detour spiritually today, but there is good news for you; tomorrow that road may not be there. Your bad situation now is temporary. It may look permanent but it is not everlasting.

(b) *It is rough and bumpy*

You will notice that it is mostly rough and bumpy. Many times you do not enjoy the ride on the detour road. This may be your story today that your life is rough and bumpy; you are no longer enjoying it. God says, hung on a little while, soon you will get to the smooth tarred road where there shall be milk and honey. Keep your hopes high. Remain focused.

I remember when we were registering our ministry; it was a rough and bumpy road. One time an officer almost insulted me. I was almost frustrated when our constitution was rejected. But the ministry remained focused until God made a way for us. Thanks be to God that we were finally registered. Your every pending issue in life will be accomplished in the same way God came in for us. All you need is to focus.

(c) *It is dusty*

On the detour you cannot have a good vision because it is dusty. This will cause you to drive at a slow speed. Sometimes, the enemy will slow your speed in your road to success. He will slow your speed in getting married, starting your own company, getting that job or in getting that acceptance letter to further your studies. Sometimes, he may even slow the growth of your church or business. But remain focussed.

(d) *It generally has a poor visibility*

There are moments you when see clearly on the detour and some moments when you do not. From this day henceforth, you will forever see at all times in the name of Jesus!

2. People

People may not harm you physically but they will distract you. Sanballat invited Nehemiah to a meeting in the plains; it was a distraction for him to abandon the work: "And I sent messengers unto them, saying, I am doing a great work, so that I cannot come down: why should the work cease, whilst I leave it, and come down to you," (Nehemiah 6:3).

3. Friends

Friends can distract you by introducing you to a new but destructive lifestyle. You may not want to offend them, so you go along with them. Many students have gone to colleges with a pure heart, but have ended up being introduced to alcohol, night clubs, drugs, seductive music, despicable videos, dishonouring games and parties that became a distraction.

There are many enemies of your progress out there. Others want your spouse, job, church, business, house, car, and etc.

Jesus was focused: "For even the Son of Man came not to be ministered unto, but to minister, and to give his life a ransom for many," (Mark 10:45).

The more focused you are the greater the momentum you will gain: "...to this end was I born, and for this cause came I into the world, that I should bear witness unto the truth," (John 18:37).

The following verses offer an illustration of the power of focus:

"The light of the body is the eye: if therefore thine eye is single, thy whole body shall be full of light," (Matthew 6:22);

"I am come that they may have abundant life," (John 10:10b);

"For this purpose the Son of God was manifested, that he might destroy the works of the devil," (1 John 3:8b);

"No man can serve two masters: for either he will hate the one, and love the other; or else he will hold to the one, and despise the other. Ye cannot serve God and mammon," (Matthew 6:24).

Bishop David Oyedepo said, "Billy Graham has stayed focused on the message of salvation God gave him from the beginning, he has not drifted an inch from it."

Billy Graham was so focused that he stayed with the message God had given him for the world.

The quickest way to do many things is to do only one thing at a time. Look at Toyota Company which has not drifted from making Toyota cars since 1933. Today, you will find Toyota almost everywhere around the globe. In South Africa, for every ten cars on the road, you will at least find eight Toyota cars.

Kentucky Fried Chicken(KFC) company has not drifted from selling chicken since 1952, they started with one branch in the USA and by 31st December 2013 they had 18, 875 total number of their outlets around the world.

This is the focus that I am talking about. Look at how they are thriving now. It was not so when they started. These people have stayed and grown in this business. In the same way, "For who hath despised the day of small things?" (Zechariah 4:10).

This is what we are lacking in this generation. We do not want to grow with ministry. We do not want to grow with success. We do not want to grow with business. We want it overnight. We want microwave breakthroughs. So many times we have "successful" people with no character. For "A gift will make room for you" but it is only character that will keep the doors open.

In 1 Kings 20:39-40 we read:

> And as the king passed by, he cried unto the king: and he said, Thy servant went out into the midst of the battle; and, behold, a man turned aside, and brought a man unto me, and said, Keep this man: if by any means he be missing, then shall thy life be for his life, or else thou shalt pay a talent of silver. And so the servant was busy *here and there*, he was gone. And the king of Israel said unto him, so shall thy judgment be; thyself hast decided it (emphasis added).

There are many people who are "here and there" who do just anything that comes their way per day. They do not know how to stay at one place. They do not know how to stay with their calling. They do not know how to stay and be content with what God has put in them. They are here and there.

If this is our attitude, chances will be very slim in us succeeding. We must stay at our jobs. We must stay with our calling. We should not be like people who want to be everywhere at once, but getting nowhere. Ever heard the monologue: "There are too many people in too many cars, in too much of a hurry, going too many directions, to get nowhere for nothing."

In order to maintain your focus and not be detoured by the devil, your enemy or your friends, you should:

(a) *Know what you want in life*

Identify your assignment and remember you cannot do everything in life. You cannot be a Jack of all trades. In 2000, I read the following from a book, "If you chase two rabbits, both will escape."

(b) *Devote your energy to it*

Paul said, "I press on." Pressing on has solved many issues. Pressing on has saved many people. Pressing on has given many pastors bigger churches. Pressing on has given many people big businesses. Do all that you can to make your vision flourish. Invest your energy and resources into it.

(c) *Resist all kinds of distraction from the devil, enemies and friends*

Remember that not all the events in life you are to attend. You need to choose at what to do and where to go at all times. Make time. Manage your time. Walk wisely, redeem the time.

(d)*Associate with people going your way*

Choose friends. Friendship is by choice and not by force. Associate with people who will add value to your life. Associate with people who will provoke you to run towards your dream.

(e)*Persevere with your focus*

You will need to realise that it will not be easy to persevere in your focus. This is why you will need to be strong and determined at what you are called to do. Hang on like a posted stamp to envelope which does not let go of envelop until it reaches its destination. Be like one. Refuse to give up. Be like Paul who said, "This one thing I do…I press towards the mark," (Philippians 3:14).

(f)*Release your faith*

All things are possible. Focused people never quit until they have accomplished their mission. Similarly, you cannot make it in life without focus. You will need focus to succeed in ministry. You will need focus to succeed in your marriage, business and in whatever you are doing in life. There is power in focus. Many people in ministry have the anointing but they have no focus. Many people can thrive in business but they lack focus. Many people can do well in politics but they lack focus, they are busy jumping from one political party to another. Many people can go very far in life but they lack focus. May the grace to be focused in life come upon you, in the name of Jesus!

Chapter 4: Power of Passion

"Jesus saith unto them, My meat is to do the will of Him that sent me, and to finish His work," (John 4:34).

This was Jesus speaking in the above verse of Scriptures. Jesus said that His meat was to do and finish the work of God. This was Jesus' food. This was His daily bread. No wonder the Lord succeeded because He was passionate about His work. His impact started then and has been growing daily. It is passion that causes men to succeed. Show me a successful man and I will show you a passionate man.

High achievers are passionate about what they do. Passion is what differentiates between success and failure. Passion is one of the dynamic forces for accomplishment in life. Passion is the force that pushes you on, in spite of all odds.

If you are going to succeed, you will need to be passionate about what you are doing. Everyone can sing, preach, or participate in sport, but it is passion that will distinguish you. It is passion that adds the flavour.

By definition, passion is a strong feeling of love for what you are doing. It is a feeling that makes you enjoy what you are doing. It is a driving force. It is what causes you to do God's work. Passion is the fuel that keeps you going. It is the energy to do what you do. It is the driving force that propels you towards accomplishment in life.

Passion is an essential tool for performance. Men of passion are men with a mission. Passion is what determines whether one will accomplish one's mission or not. I want you understand that God never gives a task without giving the passion to accomplish it. Though in itself passion does not get the job done, yet it pushes one to work at all cost.

With passion, mountains become plain grounds; obstacles give way. Passion pushes one to accomplish the impossible. Jesus was eaten up with a passion for His mission. With passion in Him, the opposition of the Pharisees was reduced to nothing. Hash conditions of living meant nothing to Him. Food was meaningless to Him. He said, "My meat is to do the will of Him that sent me, and to finish His work."

Passion is the force that pushes you on, in spite of all odds. Jesus saw the joy of accomplishment before Him and it generated passion in Him that made every obstacle lay plain. This is because God never gives a task without giving the passion to accomplishing it.

We, too, can look "…unto Jesus the author and finisher of our faith; who for the joy that was set before him endured the cross, despising the shame, and is set down at the right hand of the throne of God," (Hebrews 12:2).

Passion will compel you to take bold steps. It puts off discouragement and distraction. Passion is an inner fire that craves for results. When God created you, He put a passion inside of you for something such as business, farming, music, signing, sports, prayer, politics, education, ministry and the list is endless.

It is this passion that you enjoy doing, it is what you love to do. It is what excites you. A career should be born out of your passion. Find your passion and follow it. Wrap your career around your passion. Wrap your business around your passion. Wrap your ministry around your passion. Most of what people do is out of convenience, or to please someone or because there is nothing else to do in order to earn a living.

Passion is like food. You cannot live without it. This is why God put it in you. In this life I have seen people who have passion for cars, suits, cooking, and gardening and in many other areas. On whatever you set your passion, you will eventually succeed in it.

I watched one man on a *Dog Whisper* programme on DSTV. The man loves grooming and keeping dogs. His programme for dogs has taken him to many parts of the global. His programme has made him meet great and small people alike. Who thought a dog would cause the owners to buy Cesar an air ticket to fly to London to go and teach them how to communicate with to dogs? I believe it is the passion for animals that made this man a success story. Cesar loves what he does. He loves his work. You can see the love in him for the work he does. May you love your work to a point that it will give you joy when you do it. High achievers are passionate about what they do.

Passion is enjoyable. When you have passion for the work you do, you will enjoy it. Even when you are not paid for it, you will still enjoy doing it because that's what brings joy to you. Many people lack passion in their work. They are only working purely for money.

Look at many medical doctors and nurses in Africa – some of them lack passion. You can tell by their actions towards the patients, their look and tone of voice at the patients. Some of the medical personnel actually may contribute to the quick demise of their patients – without passion.

Jesus enjoyed His work. This is why many people were drawn to His ministry because He enjoyed doing His work. It is the love that He had for His work that drew people to Him. People always wanted to be with him. Some of them could not even lose sight of him. Other could not even go for lunch because they wanted to spend time with Him. It is the love for what you do that draws people to you.

Passion is indispensable. You cannot do without passion. Passion is necessary to sustain life. Passion is what keeps you alive. Passion is what sustains your gift and career. Passion is like the blood in your body. Without blood there can be no life. Passion is like fuel (gas) in the car. Without fuel, a car cannot move. So without passion there can be no life. Without passion, there can be no progress.

How do you know you have passion? You can know your passion by answering the following questions honestly:

(a) What do you enjoy doing?
(b) What do you flow in?
(c) I mean what comes naturally?
(d) What is in you – what one thing you do without struggle?
(e) What bears fruit in your life?
(f) Where are you most productive?
(g) Where do you bear much fruit?
(h) What can you give yourself to 100%?
(i) What can you do for nothing?
(j) What can you do without being paid?
(k) What can you do without asking for favours?

I remember in my first three years of ministry staying without having a salary. No one knew I was not on salary. I was so excited about my ministry that I blessed the people every Sunday and I did not curse them. This passion made me give myself 100% without being paid. As I did God's work with a passion, God made sure that I was taken care of. God provided all that I needed. May God provide for you as you find your passion and give yourself to it 100%!

What gives you fulfilment or satisfaction in life? What makes you feel complete? What makes you feel you are a success? What gives you happiness? What gives you pleasure?

Jesus, the Son of God, could not achieve His mission without passion. He was a passionate Master: "For the zeal of thine house hath eaten me up; and the reproaches of them that reproached thee are fallen upon me," (Psalm 69:9) and "The zeal of thine house hath eaten me up," (John 2:17).

Paul had passionate for his work: "For me to live is Christ, and to die is gain," (Romans 1:21) and "Woe is unto me, if I preach not the gospel," (1 Corinthians 9:16).

Paul had a mission, a cause. Seeing Gentiles saved was his joy. His passion knew no bounds. Paul had the fire that was burning in his bones. This was his secret to success in his ministry. Many of us have good papers for a job we are doing but we lack passion for the work. Passion never accepts failure. It sees every obstacle as a stepping-stone to the desired results. It is time you clothed with passion as with a garment.

One of the products of passion is dedication. This is the act of total surrender and devotion to a particular cause. Dedication is unreserved commitment, the giving of oneself to the pursuit of one's vision. When one knows their vision and give themselves to it with all it takes, they are said to be dedicated.

Dedication is the pathway to success. Be fully dedicated to whatever mission you have been given. Half-heartedness leads to failure.

Jesus said that His meat was to do and finish the work of God. This was Jesus' food. This was His daily bread. No wonder the Lord succeeded because He was passionate about His work. May God give you a passion for your gift and calling! May the Lord give you a zeal for your work, in the name of Jesus!

Chapter 5: Power of Discipline

"Do you not know that in a race all the runners run, but only one gets the prize? Run in such a way to get the prize," (1 Cor. 24-27).

Everyone who competes in the games goes into strict training. They do it to get a crown that will not last, but we do it to get a crown that will last forever. Therefore, I do not run like someone running aimlessly; I do not fight like a boxer beating the air.

No, I strike a blow to my body and make it my slave so that after I have preached to others, I myself will not be disqualified for the prize. Success is built on discipline. Success is a process, this means it has stages – some are easy, others are difficult, some take time but discipline is what will cause us to succeed.

Life is about creating balances because it has many good things. For instance, eating too much food is bad, sleeping too much is bad, talking too much is bad, watching TV too much is bad, and staying on phone too long is bad. Drinking too much water is bad.

What is discipline? It is the grace to exercise self-control. It is the ability to lead oneself before leading others. Discipline is self-leadership. It is an ability to master your abilities and feelings or desires. It is keeping your body under control. Discipline is the strength, appetite, and desire under control.

Discipline is keeping your appetite under control. Discipline is keeping your desires under control. Discipline is keeping your temper under control. Discipline is keeping your mouth under control. Discipline is self-management. Discipline is the strength, appetite, and desire under control.

Many people are gifted but because they lack discipline they do not go very far. The Bible says, "A gift will make room for you before great men," (Proverbs 18:16). But you will need discipline to stay on the front-line, to stay with great men. A gift will cause you to succeed but it is discipline that will keep you a success.

Paul the Apostle said: "All things are lawful unto me, but all things are not expedient: all things are lawful for me, but I will not be brought under the power of any," (1 Corinthians 6:12) and "All things are lawful for me, but all things are not expedient: all things are lawful for me, but all things edify not," (1 Corinthians 10:23). Paul is saying that I had not left his life to chance. He is saying that he did not operate by whatever came his way.

Success is built of discipline. For instance, athletes exercise discipline in what they do, eat or exercise. They are committed to what they do. Even if they feel like eating the foods that are not recommended for their health, they will not eat them because they are disciplined.

Musicians or choirs do not eat certain foods and juices because these foods affect their voices. They need discipline. Everyone can go on a diet, but it will require discipline to finally lose the weight and maintain the slim body. Some people lose weight during their diet, but they immediately gain weight when they finish their diet because they lack discipline. I want you understand that your body may be your number one enemy unless you are disciplined. It craves for food, sex, and many others. Oftentimes, you want to pray and your body wants to sleep. You want to fast and the body wants to eat. Life is about creating balances because it has many good things.

Discipline is not easy because naturally man is indiscipline. A married man will be liked by a lady in town but it will require discipline for him to stay away from such a trap. Discipline covers reading habits, what you feed your mind, what you watch, what you listen to, whether you exercises, when to fast, attend church, paying your tithe, loving your spouse every day, being faithful to your spouse and the list is endless.

After reading Mike Tyson's book, *Undisputed Truth*, I came to only one conclusion: that what brought him down was not because somebody stronger than him emerged; it was because he lacked discipline as a boxer. A gift and talent are not enough; we need discipline to make it in life. We need self-leadership. We need self-management.

For you to save money, you will need discipline. To buy your dream house and a car, you will need discipline. To rise in your ministry, you will need discipline in the areas of finances, how to relate to the opposite sex, prayer and fasting, how to avoid pride and many other areas. To rise in business, you will need discipline. To be faithful to your spouse, you will need discipline.
A disciplined person places greater value on essentials, orders his priorities, operates by schedules, functions without requiring supervision, makes the most of his or her time and has a dairy.

It took me a lot of discipline to write this book. There were many times when I was tired because I had been busy with God's work. But I had to move from time to time with my laptop and tablet in order to write something, even in-between meetings and visitations. Sometimes I had to work for 15 hours in a day just to complete a chapter or two.

Former United States President, George Washington, said, "Discipline is the soul of an army; it makes more numbers formidable, it procures success to the weak and esteem to all." Discipline can transform your life. While at Robben

Island, Nelson Mandela used to quote from *Invictus*, "I am the captain of my soul."

Success is built on discipline. Discipline is what will cause us to succeed. Having the grace to exercise self-control is what brings about success in one's life. The ability to lead oneself before leading others is what compels success in one's life. Self-leadership is what makes people make it in life. The ability to master your abilities and feelings or desires will make you successful. If you want success, learn to keep your appetite under control. Learn to keep your desires under control. Learn to keep your temper under control. Learn to keep your mouth under control.

Chapter 6: Associations

"He that *walketh* with the wise men shall be wise: but a companion of fools shall be destroyed," (Proverbs 13:20, emphasis added).

You are the sum total of those you hang around with. Somebody once said, "He who sleeps with dogs wakes up with flies." You are a product of those you associate with for good or for bad. These people shape your behaviour and model your lifestyles. They influence the way you speak, dress and carry yourself out.

Associates are powerful. They bring together people of like mindedness for a common cause.

We are influenced by associates. We human beings are social beings. We drive our joy in friendships. We always want to belong to a group, we desire to be accepted, loved and cared for. We want to be special to someone or a group of people.

The power of coming together has some common advantages:

(a) You have and share a common vision.
(b) You have almost double influence if you are two.
(c) You provide a ground for training.

(d) You share common resources.
(e) You, as teamwork, make a dream work.

Relationships in life are not optional. You need relationships for you to succeed in life. Very few people have made it alone in life. If you try to scan their success, you will discover that they had someone who stood with them or even helped them in some way. But you will need to be careful in choosing who you relate to in life on your way to success because friendship is by choice and not by force. No man is an Island. The Bible says, "...it is not good for a man to be alone..." (Genesis 2:18).

God recognized the need for the man to have another human being to relate with. The woman God made was to serve a dual purpose: Provide companionship for a man (in herself) and also to bring forth others, who could relate with him outside the home.

Two are better than one; because they have a good reward for their labour. For if they fall, the one will lift up his fellow: but woe to him that is alone when he falleth; for he hath not another to help him up (Ecclesiastes 4:9-10).

A lot of suicide stories we hear about today come from loneliness. Some suicide victims are those people who have been alone for too long. Even the Bible says that, "Iron sharpeneth iron; so a man sharpeneth the countenance of his friend," (Proverbs 27:17). We are a product of those we associate with for good or for bad.

You must have somebody that you can be in touch with, in contact with and relate to if you are to succeed in this life. You must be very selective in the friends you make because a wrong relationship may be a dream-killer and heartbreaker. A friend is like a lift (a ride), he can take you up or down. Abraham's relationship with Lot marred his vision. He could neither see nor walk into his inheritance in God: "And the Lord said unto Abram, after that Lot was separated from him, lift up now thine eyes, and look from the place where thou art…For all the land which thou seest, to thee will I give it, and thy seed forever," (Genesis 13:14-15).

Though God had told Abraham to leave his country to a land, which He would show him, yet it was not until Lot left him that God showed him the land. Also Rehoboam, King Solomon's son, fell a prey to his young friends and thereby brought about the division of the nation of Israel. The friends of the prodigal son helped him out of his plenty, into abject poverty. Similarly, Amnon's friendship with Jonadab led him into sin, which eventually took his life. The less you associate with some people, the more your life will bear fruit.

On the other hand, David's throne was preserved through his relationship with Jonathan.

Elisha's relationship with Elijah gave him a double anointing. We can therefore, deduce that there is one major thing about relationships. They can either make you or break you. Indeed, "He that sleeps with a dog, wakes up with flies." And the Bible indicts, "Be not deceived: evil communication corrupt good manners," (1 Corinthians 15:33). Therefore, be very careful in your choice of friends.

Psalm 1 clearly defines the responsibilities of a man who desires to be blessed:

> Blessed is the man that walketh not in the counsel of the ungodly, nor standeth in the way of sinners, nor sitteth in the seat of the scornful but his delight is in the law of the Lord, and in his law doth he meditate day and night. And he shall be like a tree planted by the rivers of water, that bringeth forth his fruit in his season; his leaf also shall not wither; and whatever he doeth shall prosper.

Bishop David Oyedepo once said, "A man who keeps good company will never run dry, he will never wither. He will constantly be refreshed and fulfilled." And this is supported by the Scriptures: "The blessing of the Lord, it maketh rich, and he addeth no sorrow with it," (Proverbs 10:22).

Beloved, if you want a sorrow-free progress, then seek to be blessed of God, by being highly selective of the company you keep. The choice of company is your responsibility. No relationship takes place without agreement between two parties involved.

Never become friends with someone because you both agree on negatives. Can two walk together, except they be agreed? (Amos 3:3)

Right relationships are supposed to result in progress. Wood does not sharpen iron; so any iron that relates with wood becomes blunt and the wood also suffers reduction is size, as it is chopped off. None of the parties involved in a wrong relationship profit in any way. Negative influences have the power to pull people down.

Below, I propose that three types of relationships recommended in the Bible:

1. Relationship with a superior for counselling

This is a kind of master-servant relationship. This is a relationship with people who are above you in your ministry, calling or your field. This distinction is not necessary by reason of age, but by proven results. Do not find faults with those who have gone ten steps ahead of you, instead get close to them and learn their secret to get where they are. Elijah had this type of relationship with Elisha. When other prophets were castigating Elijah, Elisha followed him, and followed through. His fellowship earned him a double portion of Elijah's anointing.

2. Relationship with colleagues

Iron sharpeneth iron; so a man sharpeneth the countenance of his friend (Proverbs 27:17). There are people with whom you engage in the same assignment, people with whom you confronted the same tasks. In this type of relationship, the people involved challenge one another to progress. In this relationship you share intimately without one dominating the other. You share heart to heart. You even reprimand one another openly. For instance, I have a companion in the ministry with whom I share testimonies and we provoke each other unto good works.

3. Relationship with a younger person (mentoring relationship)

What readily comes to mind is the relationship between Paul and Timothy and that between Jesus and His disciples. In this relationship, the older is to serve as a teacher and a leader. He sows or invests his knowledge in the younger one, who in turn receives it for his benefit. The older person is rewarded with the satisfaction he gets when the younger person performs excellently well.

Let me end by saying that you are a product of those you associate with, for good or for bad. The people you associate with shape your behaviour and model your lifestyle. These people influence the way you speak, dress and carry yourself out. Your level of success determines the level of relationships you have with others at any given time. I decree and declare that, any bad relationships you have in your life should die a natural death, in the name of Jesus!

Chapter 7: Hard Work

"Thus the heavens and the earth were finished, and all the hosts of them. And on the seventh day God ended His work which He had made; and He rested on the seventh day from all His work which he had made. And God blessed the seventh day, and sanctified it: because that in it he had rested from all his work which God created and made," (Genesis 2:1-3).

In the above text, we notice that God worked before He rested. He laid an example before us that work comes before rest. God worked hard when creating the world. We are told He never rested until He finished His work. You cannot fulfil your destiny in theory, it takes work. You are made for action.

In life we see signs of great success achieved by people who worked hard. They paid a price for the long hours they worked. They sacrificed times of pleasure and sleep in order to exert their energies towards achieving their goals in life.

Some of that hard work meant being away from friends and family and enduring with having to meet targets and deadlines. And sometimes, it meant enduring frustration, discouragement and resistance. The Bible says that, "When Jesus therefore had received the vinegar, he said, it is finished: and he bowed his head, and gave up the ghost," (John 19:3).

Work and feeding are related: "Any man that doesn't want to work, let him not eat" (2 Thess. 3:10). This scripture is talking about many people who do not want to work but they want to eat. Success requires that some obstacles be broken, some mountains be climbed, resistance be destroyed in order to overcome barriers. Success does not just happen. It has to be worked out. It has to be cultivated.

One time my spiritual father, Professor Charles Mwewa said, "Work with your hands. Do not just name and claim. Do not just confess it." I agree. And the Bible supports this assertion: "Ill-gotten treasures have no lasting value, but righteousness delivers from death. Lazy hands make for poverty, but diligent hands bring wealth," (Proverbs 10:2, 4).

To some people, work is a thorn in the flesh because they only work in order to be paid. This is why we have too many people in this world who only work well when there is a supervisor. Many people fail to accomplish their targets, they perform below average, and they are lazy or are unimpressive in their work.

Hard work is not measured by long hours spent at work, but rather by the quality of work that one produces. There should be excellence in work done.

Many people do not get promoted because they do not work hard. You secure your job through maintaining a high level of performance, handwork and excellence. Success is not for the idle. Progress in life calls for on-pressing! Every prize demands a pressing on. Hard work involves investing your abilities, strength and all you have into the pursuit of your goal. Oftentimes success will not come where you are; you have to go out looking for it. Striving for success without hard work is like trying to harvest where you have not planted. Even the Bible declares that, "The labourer is worth of his wages," (Luke 10:7). This means that for you to receive wages (salary or allowance), you must labour. You must work hard. Press forward each day. Have a list of things to do and do not knock off until you have accomplished them.

Success is not for the idle. A lazy person who wastes enormous amounts of time talking about success will win the prize of failure. The hard workers do things while the lazy sit around becoming experts at how things might be done: "By much slothfulness the building decayeth; and through idleness of the hands the house droppeth through," (Ecclesiastes 10:18). Lazy and idle people never make any head-way in life. You cannot fulfil your destiny on and in theory, it takes work. The Bible reminds us, "Seest thou a man diligent in his business? He shall stand before kings; he shall not stand before mean men," (Proverbs 22:29).

God has said, you will be the head and not the tail, you will be above only and not beneath; but the only way to get there is through hard work. Only the hardworking people will rise to the top. Only the hardworking people will stand before kings.

Look at Abraham, he was a hard worker. When God called him, He did not tell him to rear cattle. Abraham could have relaxed and said, "I am called, so I don't need to work hard; I will still make it." He would have not succeeded. But Abraham laboured and God prospered him. God can only prosper the works of your hands, not your calling, wishes and prayers. God will always prosper your calling through prospering your efforts.

Where do you think Isaac would have been if he had said to himself, "God has told me to remain in the land of the Philistines and that He will bless me here, so I don't have to work. I will sit down and wait for His blessings?" He would have waited in vain. The Bible says that, "Isaac sowed in the land:"

> The ground was tough, there was no rain in sight. But Isaac sowed in that land, and received in the same year a hundredfold: and

the Lord blessed him. And the man waxed great, and went for-ward, and grew until he became very great. For he had possession of flocks, and possession of herds, and great store of servants: and the Philistines envied him (Genesis 26:12-14).

God prospered his hard work, not his begging or idleness. Idleness attracts poverty. Idleness is sister to poverty. Invest in labour and reap the harvest, "He that tilleth his land shall be satisfied with bread: but he that followeth vain persons is void of understanding," (Proverbs 12:11).

Striving for success without hard work is like trying to harvest where you have not planted. Backbiters are idle workers. Do you know that it is only when you have stopped singing that you can know the person who misses his lines? Learn to work hard and stop spending time backbiting people. Hard work will take you to the front, where you will not be able to see people's backs. Laziness puts a man in a perpetual state of want, while the hard worker never lacks. Hard work is the path way to greatness. A hard worker presses on against all odds. Paul said, "How I kept back nothing that was profitable unto you," (Acts 20:20). It was the same Paul who also said: "Know ye not that they which run in a race run all, but one recieveth the prize? So run, that ye may obtain," (1 Corinthians 9:24).

He said run, not sit, think, wish, pray, seek help, analyse. RUN! If you will not run, then you will not have the prize. The prize is for those who will run. Beloved, there is a time to write a vision, a time to read it, share it, and a time to run with the vision. The running phase is the winning phase.

The running phase is like the planting and watering phases in farming. All the preparatory processes of the seed for planting can be likened to the writing, reading or sharing of the vision. But no matter how viable seeds are for planting, until they are actually planted and watered, no harvest is expected. If you expect a harvest, then plant like Paul and water like Apollos; that way you have opened the way for God to bring the increase. "I have planted," Paul says, and "Apollos watered; but God gave the increase," (1 Corinthians 3:6).

Yours is the task of planting and watering (running); God's business is to bring the increase. His business is to promote you. The emphasis is on the *doing* not on the writing or the reading.

> Brethren, I count not myself to have apprehended: but this one thing I do, forgetting those things which are behind, and reaching forth unto those things which

are before, I press toward the mark for the prize of the high calling of God in Christ Jesus. Let us therefore, as many as be perfect, be thus minded: and if in anything ye be otherwise minded, God shall reveal even this unto you, (Philippians 3:13-15).

The Bible also says, "Woe to them that are at ease in Zion," (Amos 6:1). Idleness attracts poverty. Success does not just happen. It must be sweated for. It must be worked for. Today, resolve to become a hard worker. Press on, be diligent. If you will not run, and if you will not work, then you will not eat, neither will you be promoted. "For even when we were with you," Paul admonishes, "this we commanded you, that if any would not work, neither should he eat," (2 Thessalonians 3:10).

The basis for increase is output. Learn to work. God will surely reward the hard worker. Those who work hard will surely obtain the prize. Those who run will definitely get the promotion and increase. So run that you may obtain! Jesus said: "I must work the works of him that sent me, while it is day: the night cometh, when no man can work," (John 9:4). Solomon the wise said: "In all labour there is profit: but the talk of the lips tendeth only to penury," (Proverbs 12:24). In the Proverbs we read, "The hand of the diligent shall bear rule: but the slothful shall be under tribute," (Proverbs 12:24). Surely, the soul of the sluggard desireth, and hath nothing: but the soul of the diligent shall be made fat!

We see that if you are not a hard worker today, you are sure to become a beggar tomorrow. "He that tilleth his land shall be satisfied with bread: but he that followeth vain persons is void of understanding," (Proverbs 12:11).

None of the common denominators to success will work unless you *do*. Success demands that you work hard. It demands that you press on for results. There is no short-cut to success. There is no such thing as an over-night success. I pray that you will be ready to sweat with joy for your success, in the name of Jesus!

Chapter 8: Price of Criticism

"And Miriam and Aaron spake against Moses because of the Ethiopian woman who he married: for he had married an Ethiopian woman,"(Numbers 12:1).

Success will not be complete without negative criticism. Success will not be complete without paying the price of criticism. Whether you like it or not, you will meet the speed humps of negative criticism on your free way to success. To succeed in life you must overcome the many efforts of others to pull you down. When you succeed in life, you will always attract erasers.

In the above-quoted verse of Scriptures, Miriam and Aaron spoke against Moses because he married an Ethiopian woman. They despised Moses and probably said, "He did not hear from God." Any genuine success will meet criticism. Genuine anointing will meet criticism. Ask the Lord Jesus and Prophet Elijah. Any genuine progress will meet criticism.

People will always have what to talk about in this life. I believe that people spoke:

1. When Noah was building the ark

May be they said, "This guy has gone

mad," because it took thirty nine years and the floods were not coming. They questioned his mental capacity. They laughed at him because it was taking too long to be completed. It took Noah forty years to build the ark. Can you imagine what society would have called him? They would have called him this and that. I can imagine how they might have called his family. I deliberately do not want to imagine how people call you or look at you, but I believe they also have a name for you. When you succeed in life, you will always attract criticism. There will always be criticism on your way to success in life.

2. When God sent Moses to Egypt

People talked. They might have also said, "Moses did not hear from God…How can God send a stammered…Are there no good people with speech eloquence somewhere…How on earth can God send a murderer to Egypt…Where was God when Moses was committing murder…This guy, Moses, doesn't even have what to offer…We know him…He is actually short tempered, isn't he?"

3. When Paul repented and started preaching the Word

"And when the barbarians saw the venomous beast hang on Paul's hand, they said among themselves, No doubt this man is a murderer, whom, though he hath escaped the sea, yet vengeance suffereth not to live," (Acts 28:4). This was after God had rescued Paul and the crew that was taking him to face Caesar in Rome.

4. Jesus

People talked also against Jesus even when he was doing God's work. Others called him a sinner, gluttonous and a winebibber, "The Son of Man came eating and drinking, and they say, Behold a man gluttonous, and a winebibber, a friend of publicans and sinners. But wisdom is justified of her children," (Matthew 11:19).

When He drove out a demon, they called Him a chief demon: "But when the Pharisees heard it, they said, this fellow doth not cast out devils, but by Beelzebub the prince of the devils," (Matthew 12:24).

When a prostitute wiped and put perfume on Jesus' feet people still talked. Even when he died on the cross, people still talked. When Jesus was raised from the dead and His tomb was found empty people said that his body was stolen at night by his disciples:

> Now when they were going, behold, some of the watch came into the city, and

shewed unto the chief priests all the things that were done. And when they were assembled with the elders, and had taken counsel, they gave large money unto the soldiers, saying, say ye, His disciples came by night, and stole him away while we slept. And if this comes to the governor's ears, we will persuade him, and secure you. So they took the money, and did as they were taught: and this saying is commonly reported among the Jews until this day" (Matthew 28:11-15).

I am sure that had Jesus lived in our times, people would still talk. They would criticize him. In fact, Jesus was killed in a conspiracy between Roman rulers and religious leaders.

5. **When Daniel was thrown into the Den of Lions**, people talked.

6. **When Joseph was put in prison in Egypt**

They might have said, "Potiphar has a lot of servants, why doesn't his wife accuse someone else…If Joseph didn't want to rape his master's wife, how come she has his garment?" Others might have said that there was no smoke without fire. And others could have said, "Now I know why Joseph like working in the house and not in the garden, all by himself."

People will always find what to talk about you. If you are building or not building people will talk. If you are single they will talk. If you marry, they will still talk. When you get married and you make a big wedding they will talk. If you do not make a big wedding, they will still talk. If you come to church, they will talk. If you do not come to church, they will still talk. If you decide to join the music ministry, they talk. If you do not join the music ministry, they will still talk.

Whatever you do in this life, you need to know that people will talk against it or about you. Even when a person has finally died and it's time for body-viewing, people will still talk about the dead body, what type of a casket he or she is put in or the quality of the tombstone used on their grave site. To succeed in life you must overcome the many efforts of others to pull you down.

Even when you decide to do nothing, so that people can have it their way, they will still find what to talk about. On your way to success, you will always have critics. Nothing in this life has ever been accomplished without controversy or criticism.

Dennis Wholey warned, "Expecting the world to treat you fairly because you are a good person is a little like expecting a bull not to attack you because you are a vegetarian."

Critics have a lot of problems themselves. They are mud-throwers; the come without clean hands. Critics usually have small minds. They are too lazy to think and work but they find it so easy to talk about others. Someone once said, "Great minds discuss ideas, good minds discuss events. Small minds discuss other people."

And our Lord chastised, "And why beholdest thou the mote that is in thy brother's eye, but perceives not the beam that is in thine own eye?" (Luke 6:41).

Bishop Charles Agyin-Asare in his book, *Pastoral Protocol*, writes:

> It has been said that in many churches it seems that the pastor cannot do anything right. No matter how sincere he may be or how hard he tries, there are always some who stand ready to find fault and criticize. Someone has described it this way:
>
> "1. If the Pastor is young, he lacks experience; if his hair is grey, he is too old for the young people.
>
> "2. If he has five or six children, he has too many; if he has none, he is setting a bad example.
>
> "3. If he preaches from notes, he has canned sermons and is dry; if his messages

are extemporaneous, he is not deep enough.

"4. If he caters for the poor in the Church, he is playing to the grandstand (trying to win favour), if he pays attention to the wealthy; he's trying to be an autocrat.

"5. If he uses too many illustrations, he is neglecting the Bible; if he doesn't include stories, he is not clear.

"6. If he condemns wrong, he is too cranky; if he doesn't preach against sin, they claim he is a compromiser.

"7. If he preaches the truth, he is too offensive; if he doesn't present the 'whole counsel of God', he is a hypocrite.

"8. If he fails to please everybody, he is hurting the church and should leave; if he does make them all happy, he has no conscience.

"9. If he drives an old car, he shames his congregation; if he buys a new one, he is setting his affection on earthly things.

"10. If he preaches all the time, the congregation gets tired of hearing, just one man; if he invites guest ministers, he is shirking his responsibility.

> "11. If he receives a large salary, he is mercenary; if he gets a small one, they say it proves he is not worth much anyway."

Critics are mud-throwers; they come with no clean hands. If you are afraid of criticism, you will die doing nothing. If you want a place in the sun, you will have to expect some blisters and some sand kicked in your face. Usually critics talk so much when they see you getting closer to the fulfilment of your destiny. The closer you get the more they talk. But they will also talk when you fail. So, succeed.

Success will not be complete without negative criticism. Whether you like it or not, you will meet the speed humps of negative criticism on your free way to success. Ignore the critics and press toward your goal, and in due season, they will change their minds.

Chapter 9: Test of Submission

"Let every soul be subject unto the higher powers. For there is no power but of God: the powers that may be are ordained by God. Whosoever therefore resisteth the power, resisteth the ordinance of God: and they that resisteth shall receive to themselves damnation. Render therefore to all their dues; tribute to whom tribute is due; custom to whom custom; fear to whom fear, honour to whom honour," (Romans 13:1-2, 7).

Somebody once whispered, "Before you can lead, you must first learn to follow." Almost everyone that is today at the top at one time they were at the bottom. Everyone who has succeeded in life at one time they first submitted to the authority. There is power in submission. Submission will lift you from the back to the top. Submission will cause you to do great things than your predecessor, ask Elisha if you don't believe me.

The Dictionary defines submission as being "under control either by God or man."Submission also means to be humble, to be meek and to surrender power to another. I want to believe that submission has to do with laying your life down to the authority. Submission is not a weakness but it is the strength under control. It is the ability to be at the service. It is the ability to follow instructions which sometimes may even be commands. Submission does not come out of convenience. Partial obedience is not enough. I have noticed that most pastors who are today doing well in ministry, first served at one time under someone else. They first submitted. Most business men and women who are doing well today at one time submitted to someone who probably even sacrificed his life to teach them business.

"Be ye followers of me, even as I also am of Christ," (1 Corinthians 11:1). What Paul is saying here is that his disciples should follow him as he followed Christ. He points it out that he also had someone that he was following. The following here is what I call submission. When you have somebody you are submitting to both at human and divine levels, you have many lessons to learn.

"Wherefore I beseech you, be ye followers of me," (1 Corinthians 4:16). Before I was ordained as a Minister of the Gospel, I first learnt how to follow. I remember starting as a Youth Chief Intercessor until I rose to a position of a pastor. My rising up was not an all-night thing. It took me some years. It was a process. The main problem in our generation is that we do not want to submit. We do not want to follow. We want to have people submit to us before we follow. This is why we have many churches, many companies, many choir groups, many political parties, and many organisations that are not causing waves at all. These days very few people are ready to submit and serve under someone. It is better to be number seven in the hierarchy where there progress, than being number one where there is none. Even at work where people are being paid, they seem to have problems in submitting to their bosses and supervisors.

"For rebellion is as the sin of witchcraft, and stubbornness is as iniquity and idolatry…" (1 Samuel 15:23). Submission is strength under control. God connects rebellion to witchcraft. He says that he who does not submit is a witch. A witch (or wizard) is a person who fails to submit. Thus, failing to submit to authority may be likened to initiation into witchcraft.

Lack of submission has destroyed marriages, divided churches, made people lose jobs, and it has taken many kids into drugs and to the streets. Lack of submission made king Soul lose his throne:

> And Saul said, Bring hither a burn offering to me, and peace offerings. And he offered the burnt offering. And it came to pass, that as soon as he had made an end of offering the burnt offering, be-hold, Samuel

came; and Saul went out to meet him, that he might salute him. And Samuel said, what hast thou done? And Saul said, because I saw that the people were scattered from me, and that thou comest not within the days appointed, and that the Philistines gathered themselves together at Michmash; and Samuel said to Saul, Thou has done foolishly: thou hast not kept the commandment of the LORD thy God, which he commanded thee: for now…..But now thy kingdom shall not continue: the Lord hath sought him a man after his own heart, and the Lord has commanded him to be captain over his people, because thou hast not kept that which the Lord commanded thee," (1 Samuel 13:9-11, 13-14).

King Saul lost his throne because he decided to disobey the Lord by not following the instructions. He did not wait for Prophet Samuel to come and offer the sacrifice. In his mind, he must have thought that he was actually doing the man of God favour. But he was disobeying the Lord. Partial obedience is not enough. God demands a complete obedience from us to everything He commands. Lot's wife also turned into a pillar of salt because she could not submit to God. She failed to follow simple instructions: "And it came to pass, when they had brought them forth abroad, that he said, Escape for thy life; look not behind thee…But his wife looked back from behind him, and she became a pillar of salt," (Genesis 19:17 and26).

Uncle Lot's wife failed the test of submission; she turned into a pillar of salt. Failing to submit to God made her lose her life. Be careful to obey all the Lord's commandments so that you do not turn into a pillar of salt. A pillar of salt has no life. It is dead. There are many Christians today who are pillars of salt. They have no life in them. They are spiritually dead because they have been disobedient to God. They are walking in rebellion. Failing to submit to authority is like initiation into witchcraft. Jonah is another man who resolved not to submit to God and have his own way. God spoke to him, "Go to Ninevah to preach My Word," but he decided to have it his way.

> Now the Word of the Lord came unto Jonah the son of Amittai, saying, Arise, go to Ninevah, that great city, and cry against it; for their wickedness is come up before me. But Jonah rose up to flee unto Tarshish from the presence of the Lord…But the Lord sent out a great wind into the sea, and there was a mighty tempest in the sea, so that the ship was like to be broken" (Jonah 1:1-4).

COMMON DENOMINATORS TO SUCCESS

We all know the story that Jonah ended up in the belly of a great fish for three days and nights. It was in the belly of a fish that God dealt with Jonah. Resolve not to be a Jonah. Disobedience is costly. If you are not careful it may cost you, life and fortune. Jonah chose death rather than obeying the Lord. He told the men in the ship to throw him into the water to die rather than going to preach to Ninevah. Poor Jonah had sunk very low. May you obey the Lord at all cost, so that you do not end up into a great wind and the mighty tempest in the sea, in the name of Jesus! May you obey the Lord so that you do not end up losing your ministry, in the name of Jesus. King Joash of Israel was asked to strike his arrow on the ground severally but stopped after the third strike. Because of his partial obedience, he could only smite Syria three times. King Joash missed a great opportunity to put his enemies on perpetual defeat:

> And he said, take the arrows. And he took them. And he said unto the king of Israel, Smite upon the ground. And he smote thrice, and stayed. And the man of God was wroth with him, and said, Thou shouldest have smitten five or six times; then hadst thou smitten Syria till thou hadst consumed it: whereas now thou shalt smite Syria but thrice," (2 Kings 13:18-19).

When we decided to begin God's work in South Africa, we sought after the face of God about where to start our ministry. In our minds we settled for Amanzimtoti, so we got a flat in this place in readiness for ministry. We also managed to reach out to one White couple thinking we are in the right place. As we kept praying, about a month later, God spoke to us separately, twice, so clearly that the land He has given us for ministry is Wentworth and not Amanzimtoti. He clearly told us that our milk and honey was in Wentworth. He told us our job was in Wentworth. We never wanted Wentworth for many reasons. But we obeyed the Lord to start the church in Wentworth. And we saw God in Wentworth. God blessed us; He gave us good families. He gave us good pastors and leaders. He supplied for us because He sent us to Wentworth. He took care of His work. We did not regret obeying the Lord. We love the church He gave us.

When you submit to God, He will lead you and provide all your needs on your way to success. Receive grace for submission both at divine and human levels, in the name of Jesus: "And Samuel said, Hath the Lord as great delight in burnt offerings and sacrifices, as in obeying the voice is better than sacrifice, and to hearken than the fat of rams," (1 Samuel 15:22).

The sin of disobedience is a terrible sin. Nothing hinders the children of God from fulfilling their purpose like disobedience does. Disobedience comes in many shades. It can take the form of refusal to keep to specific instructions, functioning in an office God has not called you to, courting a wrong relationship or operating in a place you are not meant to be in a particular time. No matter what form it takes, the truth remains that disobedience is a terrible sin in the sight of Almighty God. Disobedience compels God to turn blessings into curses, as we can see in the account of Adam and Eve.

"And unto Adam He said, because thou hast hearkened unto the voice of thy wife, and hast eaten of the tree, of which I commanded thee, saying, thou shalt not eat of it; cursed is the ground for thy sake; in sorrow shalt thou eat of it all the days of thy life," (Genesis 3:17).

Abraham was called to leave his father's house behind but he suffered the consequences of disobedience by taking Lot along with him. Who are those people the Lord expects you to have dropped but you are still hanging around? What are those things the Lord has warned you about but you are still engaging in? These are the things that will deny you the Lord's blessings.
Nothing destroys a man faster than the sin of disobedience.

Moses was so close to God that he spoke

with God mouth to mouth. But when he was told by God to speak to the rock and struck the rock instead, he was severely punished. He never got to the Promised Land.

"And the Lord spake unto Moses and Aaron, because ye believed me not, to sanctify me in the eyes of the children of Israel, therefore ye shall not bring this congregation into the land which I have given them," (Numbers 20:12). Another example is when the children do not submit to their parents, they open themselves to curses and may not live longer on earth: "Honour thy father and mother: that thy days may be long upon the land which the Lord thy God giveth thee…Honour thy father and mother …" (Exodus 20:12; Ephesians 6:2).

God commands us to honour our parents so that we may live long. In the real sense, if we do not honour our parents we shorten our lives. The secret to success is in honouring those who are older in position, responsibility and age.

It seems life is a test of submission. Here are few examples to illustrate:

1. **Elijah and Elisha**

Because Elisha submitted well to Elijah, we are told he ended up with a double unction that was upon his master. I believe Elisha had seen many weaknesses in Elijah but he still chose to submit. He must have seen the nakedness of his master but he chose to be blind and served him faithfully:

> And it came to pass, when they were gone over, that Elijah said unto Elisha, Ask what I shall do for thee, before I be taken away from thee. And Elisha said, I pray thee, let a double portion of thy spirit be upon me. And he said, Thou hast asked a hard thing: nevertheless, if thou see me when I am taken from thee, it shall be so unto thee; but if not, it shall not be so, (2 Kings 2:9-10).

Elisha followed Elijah step by step. Elisha submitted his life to Elijah. He laid his life down for Elijah his master. He followed Elijah till he got a double portion of the anointing. He persisted in following his master.

This is a spirit that Gehazi the servant of Elisha never had. He was not submissive hence he missed his opportunity to inherit a triple unction that was upon his mater. He instead inherited the leprosy from Naaman: "But Gehazi, the servant of Elisha the man of God, said, Behold, my master hath spared Naaman this Syrian, in not receiving at his hands that which he brought: but, as the Lord liveth, I will run after him, and take somewhat of him," (2 Kings 5:20).

Consider this story further:

And he said unto him, Went not mine heart with thee, when the man turned again from his chariot to meet thee? Is it a time to receive money, and to receive garments, and oliveyards, and vineyards, and to sheep, and oxen, and menservants, and maidservants? The leprosy therefore of Naaman shall cleave unto thee, and unto thy seed forever. And he went out from his presence a leper as white as snow, (2 Kings 5:26-27).

Gehazi purchased leprosy instead of triple grace because of his rebellion.

2. Moses and Joshua

Joshua worked for and submitted to Moses. Joshua never forced himself to the frontline like some of us would do. He waited and followed Moses in order to learn. I believe Joshua became a good leader because he learnt a lot from Uncle Moses: "And Joshua the son of Nun was full of the spirit of wisdom; for Moses had laid his hands upon him: and the children of Israel hearkened unto him, and did as the Lord commanded Moses," (Deut. 34:9). And also, "And the Lord said unto Moses, Take thee Joshua the son of Nun, a man in whom is the spirit, and lay thine hand upon him...And he laid his hands upon him, and gave him a charge, as the

Lord commanded by the hand of Moses," (Numbers 27:18, 23).

If you desire to be used mightily by God, you will first need to learn how to follow. You will first need to know how to submit.

3. Jesus had twelve disciples

We are told these twelve disciples followed him, ate with him and submitted unto him until their time to minister came. In fact, it was after Jesus ascended to heaven that we read about their works: "His mother saith unto the servants, whatever he saith unto you, do it," (John 2:5). Jesus obeyed His Father: "For I have not spoken of myself; but the Father which sent me, he gave me a commandment, what I should speak," (John 12:49).Whatever Jesus heard from His Father, that He did: "I can of my own self do nothing; as I hear, I Judge; and my judgment is just; because I seek not mine own will, but the will of the Father which hath sent me," (John 5:30).

In this last verse we see that the secret of Jesus' success was in doing exactly what His Father God instructed him to do. If you need success at work, do exactly as you are told. You will lose nothing in submission, if any case, you gain more when you submit. Even when you don't feel like doing the work, do it because you have been asked. Go for it with joy and soon you will obtain favour before God and man. Soon you will climb a ladder of promotion.

4. The Israelites only moved when God spoke

And the angel of God, which went before the camp of Israel, removed and went behind them; and the pillar of the cloud went from before their face, and stood behind them: "And it came between the camp of the Egyptians and the camp of Israel; and it was a cloud and darkness to them, but it gave light by night to these: so that the one came not near the other all the night," (Exodus 14:19-20).

The Lord led the Israelites by a pillar of fire and a cloud. The Israelites never made any movements till they saw these signs. Whenever there were no any signs, they pitched their tents and camped there. They could not move until God gave them a sign to do so. If God was silent for 15 days, they could still not look for a campus and make a movement. They waited upon God. You need to learn to wait upon God if you are to succeed in life.

If you really want to succeed in life, you will need to always listen to the Lord and follow His commands step by step. Do not add or subtract to the commands.

There are also some people who fail to submit, some of them decide just not to submit at all. They decide to be a problem. Let us look at some of the reasons why some people may fail to submit.

1. *Because they are more educated than the boss or supervisor*

You will need to respect your boss or supervisor no matter how much you earn or education you have. In Ministry, we don't raise leaders because of how fat their account is, we look at submission, availability and loyalty of the individual. Many gifted people have no control of their gifts, hence they are not usable in the Kingdom of God.

The fact that you have good education does not make you a boss. Having a big and good car will not make you one either. Most times education will not make you a boss. Education does not also make you wiser. In this life I have seen many educated fools. Education only gives you head knowledge. I am not against education, I like education and support it so much. I love education and one of these days I will do law and intelligence. I am just stressing a point here that submission, royalty and availability are better than education. I would rather work with a person who is willing to learn than a man with good papers and is not submissive. Sometimes this also happens when a wife earns more money than the husband. It also happens when a man earns more money than a wife.

This is not right when a woman chooses not to submit to the husband because she feels she provides for the house. I am not saying men should do nothing, am talking of submission. "Wives, submit yourselves to your own husbands, as unto the Lord," (Ephesians 5:22).

This means even if a wife has a big car, a house, a company, and more cash she must submit to a man. There are also men who look down on their wives because they earn more money or they are providing for the house. I have heard of many men who have not ever shown their pay slips to their wives. They have made sure their wives have no idea of how much they are paid. This is not good because a couple shares their success and failures together. They plan and work together. Royalty is more superior to education.

2. *Because they have a better paying job than their pastor*

> Let every soul be subject unto the higher powers. For there is no power but of God: the powers that may be are ordained by God. Whosoever therefore resisteth the power, resisteth the ordinance of God: and they that resisteth shall receive to themselves damnation. Render therefore to all their dues; tribute to whom tribute is due;

custom to whom custom; fear to whom fear, honour to whom honour," (Romans 13:1-2, 7).

You may be a manager or director at work, you are the boss at work. You are a supervisor at work, you submit to him. But when you go to church, your leader is in charge. They deserve your submission. Do not try make their job difficult, when you do this, you invite the wrath of God upon your own live.

I remember at one time I had a lady in church who was a manager at the bank. She, several times, wanted to treat me like one of her juniors at work. So one day I called her to my office and told her that when she comes to church, I am the overseer at church. Because I had an account with her bank, this bank was not hers, but she was managing it, I then told her that when I go to her bank, she is my boss there but at church I am her pastor. This is consistent with the Scriptures: "Whosoever therefore resisteth the power, resisteth the ordinance of God: and they that resisteth shall receive to themselves damnation," (Romans 13:2).

3. *They feel they are better than their leader*

Most times when we are submitting to authority, we are deceived by the enemy to think that we can do better than them. We actually point fingers at them. It is easy to pass judgment to the one on the seat. It is easy to say Cristiano Ronaldo, Lionel Messi or Neymar should have hit the ball in the left corner because you are on the grand stand.

"And why beholdest thou the mote that is in thy brother's eye, but perceives not the beam that is in thine eye," (Luke 6:41). How many politicians have promised us heaven on earth? How many politicians have promised giving us lower taxes? What happened when they got into office? Talk is cheap. It is very cheap.
I call this spirit as the *Absolom Spirit*. They divide and rule. They want sometimes to even overthrow their leaders. They get to an extent of doing anything to get to the top. If it means killing, they can kill. These types of people are so ambitious.

4. *Pride*

Some people are so big headed. They are puffed up with pride. They are mister right. They are Mrs. Right. Someone asserted, "The only reason pride will lift you up is to let you down." They feel undermined when they are rebuked or sat down to be told what to do. If you cannot submit to your supervisor because you feel he only came yesterday or you know him so well, the best you can do is to leave the company. Leave the church quickly. Resign quickly and everyone will be fine.

Some people feel they know more than their boss or leader and they fail to submit. Pray over this for you to be delivered. Or simply leave the organisation before you hurt someone.

I have told the church that I pastor many times that if there is any member who is finding difficulties in submitting to my authority, they should see me and I will gladly release them or give them a transfer letter to a church they prefer to go to. If I do this, I will be helping both the church I am pastoring and the individual failing to submit.

5. *Because a leader is younger than they are*

When sometimes people feel they have more experience than their supervisor they tend to become a problem in submitting. Because they feel they know more than him. This attitude comes from deep down their hearts which is called pride. For God's sake, what has age has to do with the work? I have seen young doctors given respect in this society. I am yet to hear that one man has refused to be operated on by a doctor who was 28 years old, but I have heard of a man refusing to submit or be corrected by a pastor who is 29 years old. I have seen taxi drivers and bankers given respect in this society but not with young pastors.

Before I married, someone in Zambia told me he likes me and enjoys my messages on radio but he cannot join or come to the church I pastored, not even to come for counselling because I was not married. I asked him what church he went to, when he told me his church. I asked him if his leaders in that church were all married. His answer was that they were not allowed, they were to stay single for the rest of their lives. Can you see how the devil blinded this man? There was much hope for me that one day I would get married and his leaders in that church had no hope at all because marriage in their church was not allowed.

6. *Because they are arrogant*

To be arrogant means making claims or pretensions to superior importance or rights. It is also an offensive display of self-importance which graduates to pride. It is to be drunk of yourself. It is to believe you are always right. People who are arrogant feel they are more important than their leaders. The Bible has a solution for arrogance: "Let nothing be done through strife or vain-glory; but in lowliness of mind let each esteem other better than themselves," (Philippians 2:3).

7. *Colour of skin*

There are also some people who find it very difficult to submit to a leader or boss because of the colour their skin. "Then Peter opened his mouth, and said, of a truth I perceive that God is no respecter of per-sons. But in every nation he that feareth him, and worketh righteousness, is accepted with him," (Acts 10:34).

God is not a racist. We are told that He accepts everyone who works righteousness. God does not show favouritism. He loves everyone and does not look at the colour of skin.

You must be above racism, too. You must grow up and submit to authority despite their colour of skin, "For there is no respect of persons with God," (Romans 2:11).

If you may, please pray this prayer, "Father Lord, please help me to be submissive in life both to you and to fellow man. I pray Lord, that I shall not be a candidate of rebellion in any way. Lord, I will fully submit at all cost, at every level, in the name of Jesus, Amen!"

Chapter 10: Getting Out of Debt

"The rich ruleth over the poor, and the borrower is a servant to the lender," (Proverbs 22:7).

I believe also that for somebody to be successful in life must learn how to handle finances. If you don't know how to handle finances, they will destroy your destiny. There is nothing evil in having money, but there is something evil when money has you.

Have you ever thought of why you are in debt? Have you scrutinized the reasons behind your debt problems? In today's world, banks are giving debts. Companies are in the business of giving debts. Individuals and clubs are giving debts. We have institutions everywhere that are mushrooming around the country because they are making money by giving debts. We have quick or fast debts with high interests. After 50 years, we become another`s slave because of quick or fast loans. When we visit shopping malls, we will find people pushing a big trolley of groceries gotten on credit. This time we can even go out for dinner on debt. We can go shopping on credit. It is like life has been made easy when in the actual sense it has been made difficult and complicated.

If debts are not handled well, they can lead to disastrous consequences in people's lives. Debts can cause your blood pressure to rise high. Debts can destroy your marriage. Debts can make you a *good* liar. I dread debts because I have seen what they have done to a one time director, businessman and nice couple.

What is debt?

A debt is a financial liability. It is a financial burden. A debt is a financial problem.
It is a financial obligation – where one borrows money or goods in order to pay back within a specified time frame, usually with interest. Many people say and think that it is evil to have debts. There is nothing evil in having debts, but there is something wrong in the way you use what you have borrowed.

Borrowing in itself is not bad what makes it bad is what you do with what you borrow Beloved, I want you to know that it is also possible to be debt free. There is no passage in the Bible that encourages us to borrow instead the Bible encourages us to be lenders.

Seven reasons why people get into debts

There are multiple factors that compel people to get into debt. Below are the causes that make people get into debts.

1. *Because they genuinely do not have money*

It is said Africans don't know how to save. One time I read a book that said: 10% must be tithe for the Lord from your income. 70% must be used at home to pay rent, bills, buy food, clothes, renovations and etc. 20% must be saved in your saving account. But many of us in Africa finish the whole income by either partying or spending anyhow. This is called poor money management. A monthly spending plan is essential, although many times people fail to plan. Somebody once said, "Failing to plan, is planning to fail." Many people don't save for emergencies. Have emergence funds. Have some money that you can fail on in an event of emergence.

2. *Because they are impatient*

"And Jacob sod pottage and Esau came from the field, and he was faint: And Esau said to Jacob. Feed me, I pray thee, with that same red pottage; for I am faint: therefore was his name called Edom. And Jacob said, Sell me this day thy birth right. And Esau said, Behold, I am at the point to die: and what profit shall this birth right do to me? And Jacob said, swear unto him: and he sold his birth right unto Jacob," (Genesis 25:29-34).

They want it now. "We know what impatience does when we embrace it. Look at Esau who sold his birth right to Jacob," (Genesis 25:33).

"And Esau said, Behold, I am at the point to die: and what profit shall this birthright do to me? And Jacob said, swear to me this day; and he swore unto him: and he sold his birthright unto Jacob." Esau wanted it now. He was too fast for a plate of soup. Many of the people of this generation are suffering from the spirit of impatience. They are the Esau's sisters and brothers. They are caring the DNA of Esau, mercy Lord! In the School of Driving they say, speed kills. This generation has been spoiled with fast foods (drive through), fast ATM's, Microwaves, cell-phones, and etc. Borrowing in itself is not bad. What makes it bad is what you do with what you borrow.

3. *Because they are not contented*

"Not that I speak in respect of want: for I have learned, in whatsoever state I am, therewith to be content (happy, satisfied, comfortable, gratified). I know both how to be abased, and I know how to abound: everywhere and in all things I am instructed both to be full and to be hungry, both to abound and to suffer need," (Philippians 4:11-12).

Not accepting they can't manage it at this hour. Many people are not content. They Have lust for materials. They have lust for money. They always want more. They are satisfied. This is microwave behaviour. It is a microwave spirit. They always want to have everything they want. They are al-ways in want of more even when you have more already.

4. *Because of medical expenses*

Expensive medical treatments make this one of the easiest ways to fall into debt. Everything to do in the medical realm costs money and usually a lot of it. On top of that Doctors and hospitals are becoming more and more impatient with people that don't pay their bills on time. Because of this, they tend to turn in patients that don't have the money to collection agencies. When you don't have the money to pay for your Doctor's visit it can be easy to put the bill on a credit card or even to take a loan out to avoid collections.

5. *Because of deficit in spending*

This occurs when spending exceeds income at any given time. This is also called overspending. An accumulated deficit becomes a debt. Not spending below your incomes or means. It's not wise to have an expenditure that is more than your income. You must learn to manage what you have. You must learn to live within your means.

6. *Because of ignorance*

Many people do not know anything about the Annual Percentage Rate (APR) on their credit cards. They have no clue as to how much they are paying for their interests on their credit card. They have no clue of the price they pay for borrowing money. They do not know the implications of "minimum payments." It is this ignorance among the general public that has propelled the rate of defaults. You must educate yourself on money matters.

If you think education is very expensive, try ignorance. People run up credit cards every day at the mall and restaurants. Companies make it easy to spend money you do not have. Buying a vehicle that you do not have the cash for also falls in the category of overspending. Going on a vacation that you cannot afford in cash is also overspending.

In life you must learn to give up on some of the extras. Limit your choices further down the road. Trim your budget to starting with the most important or needed things down to the least.

7. *Because they bank on the future*

Firstly, for instance they would say, "Let's go out and celebrate my new sales job on the credit card." But then the sales never pan out. It is also easy to get excited about the future, but we can't bank on the future happenings as we plan.

Secondly, using somebody's money thinking you will replace it tomorrow when you have your own money. This has landed a lot of people into the unplanned debts because they later found out that where they thought they would get money they never got it.

Six effects of debts

1. *It can cost your life*

Debts have power to raise high blood pressure. They can make you sick; you fail to sleep and you become a good liar. Debts have power to frustrate you to a point where you would feel you are working for nothing. Debts can affect you emotionally. They can also bring mental stress. They can even cost your marriage or relationships. Debts have power that can cause you to lose your assets. Debts can poison your success.

2. *You pay interest*

Many times it is the interest that has killed people. Sometimes you will notice that for the first one year you will be first paying interest of R300, which comes to R3600, plus now paying for your washing machine of R8000. This means you buy a machine of R5000 at R11600. They are deducting monies from your salary every month.

When you look at the business world, it is the banks and companies that give credits which make money without sweating for it. Trim your budget to starting with the most important or needed things down to the least.

3. *Can make you lose your family*

"Now their cried a certain woman of the wives of the sons of the prophets unto Elisha, saying, Thy servant my husband is dead; and thou knowest that they servant did fear the Lord: and the creditor is come to take unto him my two sons to be bondmen" (2 Kings 4:1).

It is possible to be anointed and yet in debts sinking. It is possible also to be a man of God and yet sinking in debts. Think of the above text. The only thing this man of God the prophet left for his wife to inherit was debts. What a bad testimony, beloved, if you died today, what will you leave for your children? Is it assets or debts? Can your children inherit debts or assets?

4. *Can cripple you*

Many times you cannot make personal independent decisions. It's like you becoming a slave. For example, you can't stop work when you feel like. You can change jobs when you feel like. Can you imagine in a moment you lost your job? How will you pay your debts?

5. *Can make you irresponsible*

Most of the times, monies that we borrow we don't use it wisely because we have not sweated for it. We didn't work for it. We didn't plan for it so we end up not using it wisely.

6. *Can cause to lie*

There are people who sometimes have to lie to the people or companies they owe money. They always have a lie to cover up another lie why they have not paid yet. Sometimes these liars dodge their creditors in a way you can't believe.

Some of them end up not picking their phone calls. Debts will cause you to tell your children to tell a creditor you are not at home when you are in the house.

Four points on how you should borrow

1. *Borrow only for assets or properties*

Don't borrow for personal effects such as clothes, food, shoes, carpets, a big phone, and etc. If you are to borrow for these things, then don't borrow much, borrow only something you can pay off at once on the month end. Don't let these small things control you.

2. *Do not borrow more than your income*

"For which of you, intending to build a tower, sitteth not down first, and counteth the cost, whether he have sufficient to finish it?" (Luke 14:28). You know the principle in business of income and expenditure: Don't bite more than you can chew.

As a pastor, I advise that if you are married, don't borrow alone without the consent of your partner. Go home discuss it with your partner, and look at the merits and demerits of getting the debt. Borrow something that you can pay back without struggle. "Render therefore to all their dues: tribute to whom tribute is due; custom to whom; fear to whom fear; honour to whom honour," (Romans 13:7).Remember also that, "The wicked borroweth, and payeth not again: but the righteous sheweth mercy, and giveth," (Psalm 37:21).And do not forget that, "When thou vowest a vow unto God, defer not to pay it: for he hath no pleasure in fools: pay that which thou hast vowed," (Ecclesiastes 5:4).

3. *Be sensible*

Do not borrow to make a name. Think be-fore borrowing. When you have a debt, wait to finish it before getting another one. It is unwise to keep borrowing when you know that you have a lot of debts and that it will be difficult to pay back what you are borrowing. Be reasonable. Do not think a miracle will just happen and you will be debt free. Before you borrow, think of how you will pay off this debt.

4. *Borrow according to your vision*

Do not get a loan for a car just because someone got a loan and bought a car. Do not let somebody drug you into their business or plans that will cause you spend money that you never planned for.

Seven points on how to come out of debt

1. *Decide to end this spirit:* Simply make up your mind to end this spirit, now.

2. *Make changes to your budget:* Stick to your budget when shopping or cooking. Have a monthly budget. Without a proper budget, you will not be able to track your expenses. If you write down your spending for an entire month you can see exactly where your money ends up. This is the best way to learn where you can cut some unnecessary expenses and help yourself-void debt. Be disciplined. Only buy the needs and not the wants or things for pleasure. If you want to go for school, plan first how you will pay the fees in the three years.

3. *Do not live to be a people-pleaser:* Always remember, that one day you will be asked to pay what you owe. Be yourself. If you do not have, it means you do not have. So no need to stress or push for it. Worry not about some people that will feel let down because you have not given them money or spent money on them. Do not feel that you are a saviour.

4. *Avoid spending on impulse:* Avoid shopping without a list of what you want to buy. Avoid keeping

cash money in the house or walking with it in your pocket or hand bag. Avoid the tradition and competition/be yourself. For example, do not buy clothes because everyone else buys clothes on Christmas; or because everyone else is having a brail (BBQ)' or because everyone else is driving; or because everyone else is having a wedding; or because everyone else is going out.

Do not let events control you. It is important to make thoughtful decisions about where and when to spend your money. Do not spend money without thinking. If you want to make an investment, make sure you do not make a wrong decision.

5. *Grow up*: "Lying lips are abomination to the Lord: but they that deal truly are his delight," (Prov. 12:22). Mature. Know what you want to achieve. Ask yourself what you would leave for your children if you died. You must purpose to live a clean life. You must purpose not to leave debts. In 2 Kings 4:1, we see the prophet (man of God) leaving debts for his wife when he died. The debtors were now coming to get his sons in place of what he owed them.

6. *Live within your means*: Be real to yourself. Spend within your means. Live within your incomes. Live within what you can manage.

In the Zambian Nyanja language there is

a proverb that says, *Anione anione, anankalapansimbi yokupya*. This means in English: "He who does things to be seen, ends up sitting on a hot stove." Outsiders may be afraid of you and think you have a lot of money, when in the actual sense you are sitting on a hot stove. Meanwhile, there is pressure that only you alone know.

Another Zambian proverb in the Bemba language says, *Ing'anda baikumbwa umutenge*. In English it may be translated as, "You can only admire a house by looking at it from the roof, because you don't know what is inside." Understand that you are not everyone. Understand that you are to live according to the level of your income.

7. *Small savings matter.* If you want to avoid unwanted debt, try to be prepared for unexpected expenditures by saving some money. If you have decent savings in place you can use it for emergences like severe illness, job-loss, tire bursts, car service, transport to go and attend a funeral of your relative, money to buy foods, clothes, casket at the funeral etc. believe me, no one ever regrets saving money for emergencies. My advice is that you always save at least a 10 percent of your monthly incomes.

In the today's world we have had easy access to debts. Banks are giving debts.
Companies are in the business of giving debts.

Individuals and clubs are giving debts. We have institutions everywhere that are mushrooming around the country because they are making money through giving debts. We have quick or fast debts, quick or fast loans.

If we are to come out of debts, we must learn to budget, save emergency funds, and living within our means. You will need to live within your means. You will need to be in your own world. Live according to your plan and income. There is hope for you that you can make things right. I see you making a decision to come out of debt and becoming a free man.

Chapter 11: God Factor

It is written in Psalm 127:1, "Except the Lord build the house, they labour in vain that build it: except the Lord keep the city, the watchman waketh but in vain."

There is a God factor to success in life. God must be the centre of your success. True success is found in God. Anything you achieve outside God is not true success. Any success you get outside of God may not stand the fire. It is like smoke, for tomorrow it may not be there.

As it is written: "The blessing of the Lord, it maketh rich, and he addeth no sorrow with it," (Proverbs 10:22).

Allow me to contextualize the above text in my own version, this scripture is actually saying, "The success of the Lord, it maketh rich, and He addeth no sorrow with it." Anything you achieve outside of God may not be true success. The success of the Lord is sorrow free. It is free from tension and many problems. Because, except the Lord builds your success, your labour may be in vain, and except the Lord keeps your success, you may watch but in vain.

Moses advises Joshua: "This book of the law shall not depart out of thy mouth; but thou shalt meditate therein day and night, that thou mayest observe to do according to all that is written: for then thou shalt make thy way prosperous, and then thou shalt have good success," (Joshua 1:8). Being born again is a prerequisite for a good success in life. This is what qualifies one to be successful. Jesus said: "I am the way, the truth and life; no man cometh unto the Father but by me," (John 14:6). No man has an inheritance in a family to which he does not belong. In the same way, without being born again, you do not have an inheritance in Christ. This is why I believe Jesus said, "Jesus answered and said unto him, verily, verily, I say unto thee, except a man be born again, he cannot see the kingdom of God," (John 3:3).

It is pointless to claim you have success when you do not have Christ in you. Because you see, money will not take you to heaven. Hard work without God is useless.

Whatever you own will not take you to heaven. Success without God may lead one to premature death and even madness. Nothing is substitute for your redemption if you want true success in your life: "Every good gift and every perfect gift is from above, and cometh down from the Father of lights," (James 1:17).

Every good and perfect success comes from God. When God gives you success, He will sustain it. Many of man's successes are but for a moment. It doesn't outlive a man, it dies with a man. Today we are reaping Abraham's blessing because his success was all because of God who was in His life.

Examples of men with a God-factor

1. Joseph

"And the Lord was with Joseph, and he was a prosperous man; and his master saw that the Lord was with him, and that the Lord made all that he did to prosper in his hands. Joseph found grace in his sight, and he served him: and he made him overseer over his house, and all that he had he out into his hand," (Genesis39:2-4).

It was because of God that Joseph succeeded in life. Let's look at few things that we see in the life of Joseph:

(a) *The Lord was with him*

"And the Lord was with Joseph…" (Genesis 39:2a).

God was with Joseph. God made sure that He was with Joseph. Joseph also made sure He did what pleased the Lord for God to be with him. Joseph knew the God factor in life. When God is with you, your success is guaranteed. And in another place, it is again written, "But the Lord was with Joseph…" (Genesis 39:21a).

(b) *Joseph was a prosperous man*

"...and he was a prosperous man..." (Genesis 39:2b).

It is pointless to claim you have success when you do not have Christ in you. Joseph prospered not because he was a wise-man but because God was with Him. When God is with you, He will make sure you always succeed because He can't fail. Whatever Joseph did, prospered: "...and the Lord made all that he did to prosper," (Genesis 39:3b).

Consider the following verse: "Blessed is the man that walketh not in the counsel of the ungodly, nor standeth in the way of sinners, nor sitteth in the seat of the scornful, but his delight is in the law of the Lord; and in his law doth he meditate day and night. And he shall be like a tree planted by the rivers of water, that bringeth forth his fruit in his season; his leaf also shall not wither; and whatsoever he doeth shall prosper," (Psalm 1:1-3). Whatever he doeth shall prosper! You only make your way prosperous once you find delight in the ways of the Lord.

(c) *Joseph found grace in Potiphar's house*

"And Joseph found grace in his sight...." (Genesis 39:4a).

It was because God was with Joseph that Joseph found grace in Potiphar's sight. When God is with you, He grants you grace in the eyes of every man. He grants you favour in the sight of those who are in the place of influence. This is its not biblical and wise to chase for divine connection with the great when you have not set your mind on God.

"But the Lord was with Joseph, and shewed him mercy, and gave him favour in the sight of the keeper of the prison," (Genesis 39:21). Joseph succeeded in life because God was with him. If God was not with him, he would have not made it to the top.

(d) *Joseph was made an overseer*

"And he made him an overseer over his house, and all that he had put into his hand," (Genesis 39:4b).

Joseph was made an overseer in Potiphar's house not because he was so educated or he had good connections. It was because God was with him. This is what God does when He is with you. He will make sure you are made an overseer. An overseer is a boss, a manager and a supervisor. With God success is assured. He will make sure you climb a ladder of success. Even where you don't know anyone to favour you, God will make a way for you to succeed.

2. Father Moses

"And he said unto Him, if thy presence go not with me, carry us not up hence," (Exodus 33:15).

Father Moses knew that his success was only guaranteed in the Lord. He knew that his labour would be in vain if he went to face Pharaoh in his strength. This is why the Magicians of Egypt said, "This is the finger of God upon Moses," (Exodus 31:18).

God gave success to Moses before Pharaoh. May God give you success as you walk with Him, in the Name of Jesus!

3. Three Hebrew boys

"And these three men, Shadrach, Meshach, and Abednego, fell down bound into the midst of the burning fiery furnace. Then Nebuchadnezzar the king was astonished, and rose up in haste, and spake, and said unto his counsellors, did not we cast three men bound into the fire? They answered and said unto the king, True, O king. He answered and said, Lo, I see four men loose, walking in the midst of fire, and they have no hurt; and the form of the fourth is like the Son of God," (Daniel 3:23-25).

God gave the boys protection until they succeeded. When God gives you success, He will protect you on the way through. Jesus appeared in the fire with the three Hebrew boys because they walked with Him. The secret to success is walking with God.

4. Jesus

"How God anointed Jesus of Nazareth with the Holy Ghost and with power: who went about doing good, and healing all that were oppressed of the devil; for God was with him," (Acts 10:38).

The above text tells us that because God was with Jesus:

(a) Jesus was anointed with the Holy Ghost and power

When God is with you, He will anoint you with the Holy Ghost and power in order for you to function. He cannot give you a work that you don't have what it takes to do it. He will always give you the anointing to manage the work.

(b) *Jesus went about doing good*

God made sure that the nature of Jesus' work was good. When God is on your side whatever you do will be good. Even when the enemy tries to do any evil to you, God will turn it for your good.

"You meant it for evil but God turned it for good," (Genesis 50:20) declares.

(c) *Jesus went healing all those who were oppressed of the devil*

When God is with you, He will use you greatly to do the usual. He will use you to be an answer to the society and the poor.

There are many other examples I would want to show you of men and women in the Bible that succeeded with the help of God. But because of not having enough ink and paper, I will end here.

True Christian success has a basis on God. It has a genesis in God. It has a foundation in God. Having God in your life is the easiest way to success. It's too risk for you to strive for success without God on your side. I charge you to make God the centre of your life, because He will sustain and drive you to ultimate Christian success.

Index

A

Abraham Lincoln 20
Absolom Spirit..... 95
accomplished. 11, 32, 38, 65, 75
Amanzimtoti 85
ambition 5
arrogance 97
Associations 55
athletes 50

B

bankon the future .. 105
Be sensible 109
Bible .. 2, 13, 50, 56, 58, 59, 63, 64, 65, 66, 69, 77, 97, 100, 122
Bishop Charles Agyin-Asare 76
blood 45, 100, 105
born again 116
Borrow only for assets or properties 108
breakthroughs 35
budget . 10, 104, 106, 110, 113

C

cause to lie 107
Charles Mwewa ... 22, 64
Christ 80
church. 9, 19, 33, 34, 51, 75, 77, 85, 94, 96, 97
circumcision 8
colour their skin ... 98
commandments 6, 83
common 1, 23, 55, 56, 70
compassion 26
Correct timing 15
cripple you 107
criticism 71
crown 49

D

Daniel 74
death . 11, 12, 61, 64, 84, 116
debt 99, 100, 103, 104, 108, 109, 110, 112, 113

dedication 47
deficit in spending ... 103
depend on God ... 25
destiny 11, 30, 63, 65, 78, 99
discipline 49
Disobedience 84
distraction .. 31, 33, 34, 37, 43
divine connection 119
Divine guidance 12
Do not borrow more than your income 108
do not have money .. 101
doing 68
dream .. 1, 3, 6, 7, 11, 15, 21, 38, 52, 56, 57
dusty 32

E

Elijah and Elisha... 87
enemies 34
Esau 101

F

failure.. 1, 19, 20, 21, 22, 23, 24, 25, 26, 27, 30, 41, 47, 65
faith 6, 13, 21, 38, 42
Faithful 13
finger of God 120
Focus 29
food .. 41, 43, 47, 49, 51, 101, 108
Friends 33
Friendship 38
fulfilment 46

G

Gehazi 88
Gentiles 46
George Muller 6
George Washington 52
God 4
God factor 115
grace 4, 24, 25, 39, 49, 53, 85, 89, 117, 118, 119
Grow up 111

H

Half-heartedness .. 47

hard work 63
harvest 65, 67, 68
Hitler 5
humble 26

I

ignorance 104
improve 25
increase 9, 68, 69
iniquity 81

J

Jack of all trades .. 37
Jacob 101
Jerusalem 30, 31
Jesus 8, 11, 13, 14, 24, 29, 33, 34, 39, 41, 42, 44, 46, 47, 60, 61, 64, 69, 70, 71, 73, 74, 84, 85, 90, 98, 116, 120, 121, 122
Jews 6, 10, 74
Jonah 83
Joseph 74

K

King Joash 84

L

labour 65
Laziness 67
learning curve 24
life 4
lose your family 106
love 8, 26, 30, 34, 41, 43, 44, 85, 92

M

manufacturer 7
medical expenses 103
Mike Tyson 51
ministry ... 1, 2, 9, 23, 25, 29, 32, 35, 38, 43, 44, 46, 47, 52, 59, 60, 75, 80, 84, 85
mischief 19
Mistakes 25
money 99
Moses 72
Moses and Joshua 89
Musicians 51

N

Naaman 89
Nelson Mandela ... 53
Ninevah 84

Noah 71
not contented 102

P

Passion 41
path 16, 67
Paul 72
Paul Galvin 21
People 33
people-pleaser 110
Persevere 38
PHDs 5
pillar of fire and a cloud 91
pillar of salt 82, 83
poor visibility 33
poverty 67
prayer 43, 52, 98
pride 96
privileges 20
product 7
progress .. 30, 34, 45, 59, 60, 71, 81
Promised Land ... 12, 14, 87
prophecy 7
prophet 4, 7, 107, 111
prosper 13, 58, 66, 117, 118

R

rebellion 81
Relationship with a superior 59
Relationship with a younger person 60
Relationship with colleagues 60
Relationships 56
Run 68

S

Sanballats 31
Sangoma 11
satisfaction 46
Scriptures 3, 8, 41, 58, 71, 94
Security of destiny 16
self-leadership 49
self-management .. 52
Sir Watts 24
slothfulness 65
Son of Man 34, 73
spouse 22, 34, 51, 52
stubbornness 81
submission 79

success...1, 9, 10, 19, 21, 22, 23, 24, 25, 26, 27, 29, 30, 32, 35, 41, 44, 46, 47, 50, 52, 53, 56, 61, 63, 65, 67, 70, 71, 72, 75, 78, 85, 87, 90, 93, 106, 115, 116, 117, 118, 119, 120, 121, 122

T

talent 1, 36, 52
temporary road 31
the cross 42, 73
The Devil 30
Three Hebrew boys 120
twelve disciples 90

U

Undisputed Truth 51

V

vision 1, 3, 4, 5, 6, 7, 8, 10, 11, 12, 15, 16, 29, 30, 32, 37, 47, 55, 57, 68, 109

W

Wentworth 85
wisdom 73

Y

You pay interest 106

Z

Zambia 97
zeal 46

Notes

www.ingramcontent.com/pod-product-compliance
Lightning Source LLC
Chambersburg PA
CBHW061443040426
42450CB00007B/1182